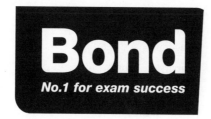

Verbal Reasoning

Assessment Papers

9–10 years

Book 2

OXFORD
UNIVERSITY PRESS

Great Clarendon Street, Oxford, OX2 6DP, United Kingdom

Oxford University Press is a department of the University of Oxford.
It furthers the University's objective of excellence in research,
scholarship, and education by publishing worldwide. Oxford is
a registered trade mark of Oxford University Press in the UK and in
certain other countries

British Library Cataloguing in Publication Data
Data available

978-0-19-277744-7

10 9 8 7 6 5 4 3 2 1

Paper used in the production of this book is a natural, recyclable
product made from wood grown in sustainable forests.
The manufacturing process conforms to the environmental
regulations of the country of origin.

Printed in China

Acknowledgements

The publishers would like to thank the following for permissions to
use copyright material:

Page make-up: OKS Prepress, India
Cover illustrations: Lo Cole

Although we have made every effort to trace and contact all
copyright holders before publication this has not been possible in all
cases. If notified, the publisher will rectify any errors or omissions at
the earliest opportunity.

Links to third party websites are provided by Oxford in good faith
and for information only. Oxford disclaims any responsibility for
the materials contained in any third party website referenced in
this work.

Before you get started

What is Bond?

This book is part of the Bond Assessment Papers series for verbal reasoning, which provides a **thorough and progressive course in verbal reasoning** from ages six to twelve. It builds up reasoning skills from book to book over the course of the series.

What does this book cover and how can it be used to prepare for exams?

Verbal reasoning questions can be grouped into four distinct groups: sorting words, selecting words, anagrams, coded sequences and logic. *Verbal Reasoning 9–10 Book 1 and Book 2* practise a wide range of questions appropriate to the age group drawn from all these categories. The papers can be used both for general practice and as part of the run up to 11+ and other selective exams. One of the key features of Bond Assessment Papers is that each one practises **a very wide variety of skills and question types** so that children are always challenged to think – and don't get bored repeating the same question type again and again. We believe that variety is the key to effective learning. It helps children 'think on their feet' and cope with the unexpected: it is surprising how often children come out of verbal reasoning exams having met question types they have not seen before.

What does the book contain?

- **15 papers** – each one contains 65 questions.
- **Tutorial links throughout** - 📖 – this icon appears in the margin next to the questions. It indicates links to the relevant section in *How to do 11+ Verbal Reasoning*, our invaluable subject guide that offers explanations and practice for all core question types.
- **Scoring devices** – there are score boxes in the margins and a Progress Chart on page 60. The chart is a visual and motivating way for children to see how they are doing. It also turns the score into a percentage that can help decide what to do next.
- **Next Steps Planner** – advice on what to do after finishing the papers can be found on the inside back cover.
- **Answers** – located in an easily removed central pull-out section.

How can you use this book?

One of the great strengths of Bond Assessment Papers is their flexibility. They can be used at home, in school and by tutors to:
- set **timed formal practice** tests – allow about 40 minutes per paper. Reduce the suggested time limit by five minutes to practise working at speed.
- provide **bite-sized chunks** for regular practice
- **highlight strengths and weaknesses** in the core skills
- identify **individual needs**
- set **homework**
- follow a complete 11+ preparation strategy alongside *The Parents' Guide to the 11+* (see overleaf).

It is best to start at the beginning and work though the papers in order. If you are using the book as part of a careful run-in to the 11+, we suggest that you also have two other essential Bond resources close at hand:

How to do 11+ Verbal Reasoning: the subject guide that explains all the question types practised in this book. Use the cross-reference icons to find the relevant sections.

The Parents' Guide to the 11+: the step-by-step guide to the whole 11+ experience. It clearly explains the 11+ process, provides guidance on how to assess children, helps you to set complete action plans for practice and explains how you can use the *Verbal Reasoning 9–10 Book 1* and *Book 2* as part of a strategic run-in to the exam.

See the inside front cover for more details of these books.

What does a score mean and how can it be improved?

It is unfortunately impossible to predict how a child will perform when it comes to the 11+ (or similar) exam if they achieve a certain score on any practice book or paper. Success on the day depends on a host of factors, including the scores of the other children sitting the test. However, we can give some guidance on what a score indicates and how to improve it.

If children colour in the Progress Chart on page 60, this will give an idea of present performance in percentage terms. The Next Steps Planner inside the back cover will help you to decide what to do next to help a child progress. It is always valuable to go over wrong answers with children. If they are having trouble with any particular question type, follow the tutorial links to *How to do 11+ Verbal Reasoning* for step-by-step explanations and further practice.

Don't forget the website...!

Visit www.bond11plus.co.uk for lots of advice, information and suggestions on everything to do with Bond, the 11+ and helping children to do their best.

Paper 1

Underline the pair of words most similar in meaning.

Example   come, go   roam, wander   fear, fare

1 test, exam   learn, read   science, mathematics

2 melt, fade   dirty, clean   rot, decay

3 drink, water   eat, consume   join, attract

4 hard, rough   black, red   light, pale

5 extend, enlarge   side, back   easy, late

5

Underline the two words, one from each group, which are the most opposite in meaning.

Example   (dawn, early, wake)   (late, stop, sunrise)

6 (once, then, here)   (never, open, now)

7 (large, hairy, wild)   (tiny, untidy, cold)

8 (stretch, easy, loose)   (pull, tight, take)

9 (awake, dark, hollow)   (solid, open, confused)

10 (second, minute, first)   (hour, third, final)

5

Complete the following sentences by selecting the most sensible word from each group of words given in the brackets. Underline the words selected.

Example   The (children, books, foxes) carried the (houses, books, steps) home
from the (greengrocer, library, factory).

11 The (farmer, teacher, shopkeeper) asked the (men, sheep, children) to eat their
(shoes, lunches, flowers) sensibly.

12 Don't (try, remember, forget) (swimming, jumping, running) in such a strong
(puddle, tide, night).

13 Why are those (boats, trees, cows) standing (huddled, wide, near) together in the
(shop, ground, field)?

14 The (team, colour, home) scored a (peach, ball, goal) to win the (last, match, run).

15 James (rubbed, used, whisked) the (jumper, dessert, pencil) with a
(hose, pound, fork).

5

Underline the two words which are made from the same letters.

Example TAP PET <u>TEA</u> POT <u>EAT</u>

16	SHADES	SHADOW	SHIELD	DASHES	SHINES
17	STARS	TEARS	STATE	TEASE	RATES
18	PEARS	STEER	SPEAR	PLEAT	TREAT
19	SHOVE	FLASH	FLESH	SHAVE	SHELF
20	LATER	STEEL	TRAIL	STEAL	LEAST

 5

Find the four-letter word hidden at the end of one word and the beginning of the next word. The order of the letters may not be changed.

Example The children had bats and balls. <u>sand</u>

21 He decided to have breakfast early that morning. _____

22 The garage mechanic repaired her new car promptly. _____

23 'Don't I get a hello any more?' asked Mum. _____

24 He put a larger dynamo onto the old bicycle. _____

25 This was a radical move for Professor Shirka. _____

 5

Find the letter which will end the first word and start the second word.

Example peac (<u>h</u>) ome

26 mal (___) scape

27 hos (___) eat

28 see (___) ade

29 tea (___) ota

30 soa (___) ure

 5

Find and underline the two words which need to change places for each sentence to make sense.

Example She went to <u>letter</u> the <u>write</u>.

31 The motor lake roared across the calm boat.

32 You thought that she couldn't hear I.

33 The mechanic was repaired by the car.

34 Where is you think she do going?

35 The caged sea roared like a angry lion.

5

2

Fill in the missing letters. The alphabet has been written out to help you.

A B C D E F G H I J K L M N O P Q R S T U V W X Y Z

Example AB is to CD as PQ is to RS.

36 JK is to LM as RS is to _____.

37 GE is to DB as AY is to _____.

38 EF is to HI as KL is to _____.

39 T5 is to V7 as X9 is to _____.

40 XX is to YA as BB is to _____.

B 23

5

Which one letter can be added to the front of all of these words to make new words?

B 12

Example care   cat   crate   call

41 ___old   ___read   ___ait   ___rand

42 ___and   ___old   ___oup   ___hare

43 ___otion   ___ay   ___ould   ___ore

44 ___our   ___outh   ___oung   ___ell

45 ___live   ___bate   ___bout   ___mend

5

Fill in the crosswords so that all the given words are included. You have been given one letter as a clue in each crossword.

B 19

46
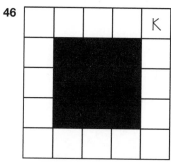

tiles, shark, start, knees

47
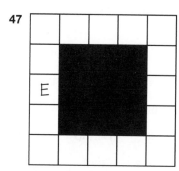

tries, fresh, front, heads

48
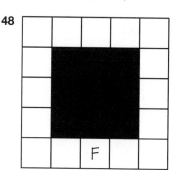

tufts, elves, aloft, above

49
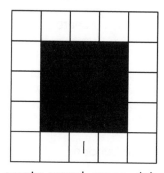

empty, round, rupee, daisy

50

		U		
	■	■	■	
	■	■	■	
	■	■	■	

grand, gruel, dough, laugh

B 24

If the code for TRAVEL is $ * : £ − &, what are the codes for the following words?

51 REAL _____

52 TEAR _____

53 LEAVE _____

If the code for TRAIN is @ < ? > !, what do these codes stand for?

54 @ ? < _____

55 @ ? > ! @ _____

B 7

Underline the one word which **cannot be made** from the letters of the word in capital letters.

Example STATIONERY   stone   tyres   ration   <u>nation</u>   noisy

56 DETAILED   late   dated   laid   leaded   tamed

57 SUPERVISE   revise   revue   vipers   every   serve

58 COMPLICATED   laced   matted   calmed   placed   malice

59 MANAGEMENT   games   agent   magenta   meant   game

60 TIDEMARK   taker   dream   dimmer   marked   armed

61 ESTRANGE   gears   snare   grates   earns   groan

B 25

A music festival is being held in London. To get there, you would have to travel 12 km from Wiston. If you lived in Bridgeworth you would have to go 4 km further than from Wiston but 6 km less than from Hambury. From Fettle it is only half the distance to London that it would be from Hambury.

62 Which town is closest to London? _____

63 Which town is furthest from London? _____

64 How far is Bridgeworth from London? _____

65 How much further from London is Wiston than Fettle? _____ 4

Now go to the Progress Chart to record your score!   Total 65

Paper 2

Underline the two words in each line which are most similar in type or meaning.   B 5

| **Example** | dear | pleasant | poor | extravagant | expensive |

1 withdraw   build   retrain   construct   demolish

2 destroy   remove   put   place   lie

3 attempt   adjust   leave   reveal   try

4 starting   grave   thoughtful   ending   serious

5 easy   correct   wrong   complex   effortless   5

Underline the pair of words most opposite in meaning.   B 9

Example cup, mug   coffee, milk   hot, cold

6 flat, even   false, true   strange, wild

7 continuous, ended   allowed, admitted   flaky, dry

8 quick, swift   plain, elegant   hunch, guess

9 wet, damp   truth, honesty   criticise, praise

10 cured, improved   full, complete   well, ill   5

Underline the two words, one from each group, that go together to form a new word. The word in the first group always comes first.   B 8

Example (hand, green, for)   (light, house, sure)

11 (good, high, flat)   (friend, out, mate)

12 (cold, wet, at)   (put, tack, pie)

13 (for, try, down)   (lawn, late, sake)

14 (on, out, way)   (fold, cry, lie)

15 (left, in, far)   (vest, way, out)   5

5

Find the three-letter word which can be added to the letters in capitals to make a new word. The new word will complete the sentence sensibly.

B 22

Example   The cat sprang onto the MO.   U̲S̲E̲

16–17 Jane's BHER told her that his cat had FOLED him to school that day. ——— ———

18–20 Her CLASSE told Seena she should TELEPH
her mother to come and collect her IMMEDILY. ——— ——— ———

5

Find the four-letter word hidden at the end of one word and the beginning of the next word. The order of the letters may not be changed.

B 21

Example   The children had bats and balls.   s̲a̲n̲d̲

21 He reached the deadline in time.   —————

22 The rusty old door opened with a scary creak.   —————

23 Tara reminded her mother that Monday was a holiday. —————

24 In winter the hen would stop laying eggs.   —————

25 The prisoner shouted his plea several times.   —————

5

Change the first word into the last word, by changing one letter at a time and making a new, different word in the middle.

B 13

Example   CASE   C̲A̲S̲H̲   LASH

26 PUSH   ———   POST

27 REAR   ———   SEAT

28 LAST   ———   HOST

29 FINE   ———   MINT

30 STAR   ———   SNAG

5

Complete the following sentences by selecting the most sensible word from each group of words given in the brackets. Underline the words selected.

B 14

Example   The (children, books, foxes) carried the (houses, books, steps) home
from the (greengrocer, library, factory).

31 When will we (land, address, arrive) in our (fresh, artistic, holiday) (conservatory, resort, canvas)?

32 Which (way, man, frog) do we (eat, go, hunt) to get to the (theatre, lunch, flower)?

33 The (quiet, hungry, learner) driver kept (eating, speeding, stalling) the car's (supper, engine, wheels).

34 In the (hungry, spotted, old) (bush, castle, wagon) lived a noble (king, brick, bathroom).

35 In (art, mathematics, history) we learn about (dance, football, graphs) and (television, numbers, drawing).

Choose two words, one from each set of brackets, to complete the sentences in the best way.

> **Example** Smile is to happiness as (drink, <u>tear</u>, shout) is to (whisper, laugh, <u>sorrow</u>).

36 Monday is to Wednesday as (Tuesday, Thursday, Sunday) is to (Monday, Wednesday, Saturday).

37 Flight is to aircraft as (walk, trial, sailing) is to (car, ship, automobile).

38 Rim is to plate as (picture, shore, water) is to (lake, painting, drink).

39 Uncertain is to sure as (tired, restricted, grateful) is to (late, unlimited, trained).

40 Trivial is to insignificant as (considerate, unstable, trembling) is to (generous, prudent, unkind).

Fill in the crosswords so that all the given words are included. You have been given one letter as a clue in each crossword.

41
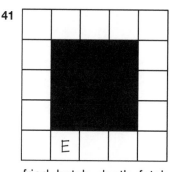
fried, hatch, death, fetch

42
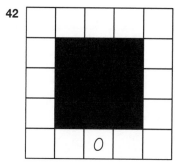
story, diary, grind, goats

43
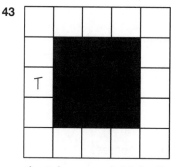
elect, brown, night, bathe

44
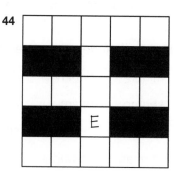
irate, after, forge, later

45

chest, metre, mocha, pleat

Give the missing numbers in the following sequences.

 B 23

    Example 2   4   6   8   <u>10</u>   <u>12</u>

46   62   58   ___   50   46   ___

47   7   9   12   ___   ___   27

48   1   5   3   ___   5   9   ___

49   25   20   30   ___   35   ___

50   2   4   8   ___   32   ___

 5

If the code for BALLISTIC is < > ? ? £ % X £ +, what are the codes for the following words?

B 24

51 BALLS   _____

52 LIST   _____

53 STAB   _____

What do these codes stand for?

54 £ ? ?   _____

55 + > ? ?   _____

 5

Underline the one word in each group which **cannot be made** from the letters of the word in capital letters.

B 7

    Example STATIONERY   stone tyres ration <u>nation</u> noisy

56 REMAINDER   mined   denim   rider   married   drained

57 WORKMANSHIP   shrimp   prism   hawks   plank   sharp

58 TELEVISION   version   invites   seven   event   list

59 ARRANGEMENT   remnant   manager   anger   garment   nearest

60 PERSONAL   snare   polar   salon   plain   loans

5

Anna supports France and England. Liam supports Wales and England. Malik does not support Scotland but supports Wales. Donna supports Scotland, England and Brazil. David hates football.

B 25

61 How many teams do Donna and Malik support together? _____

62 Which country has the most supporters? _____

2

Eleanor lives 5 km from school. Su lives nearest to school. Francesca lives 2 km closer than Eleanor, who lives 4 km further from the school than Su. Robert lives 1 km further than Su.

B 25

63 Who lives furthest from school? _____

64 How much nearer to school is Su than Francesca? _____

2

Charlotte is five years older than Lianne, who is four years younger than Lily. Lily is one year older than Ellie, who is three years older than Jessica. Ellie is 10.

B 25

65 Which two girls are twins? _____

1

Now go to the Progress Chart to record your score! **Total** 65

Paper 3

Underline the word in the brackets closest in meaning to the words in capitals.

B 5

Example	UNHAPPY	(unkind death laughter <u>sad</u> friendly)

1 PULL, TUG   (drop   drag   eat   kick   boat)

2 WASP, BEETLE   (butterfly   horse   salmon   snake   mouse)

3 POMEGRANATE, TOMATO   (sprout   lettuce   apple   onion   beetroot)

4 CONTRACT, PACT   (agreement   code   shrink   invitation   signature)

5 WALES, FINLAND   (London   Essex   Leeds   Russia   Kent)

5

Underline the two words, one from each group, which are the most opposite in meaning.

B 9

Example   (dawn, <u>early</u>, wake)   (<u>late</u>, stop, sunrise)

6 (wonder, love, try)   (find, heat, hate)

7 (hard, fine, soft)   (furry, effortless, light)

8 (reject, refill, waste)   (conserve, rubbish, useful)

9 (fair, honest, closed)   (just, truthful, dark)

10 (reduce, infinite, counted)   (endless, hourly, limited)

5

Find the letter that will end the first word and start the second word.

Example   peac (h) ome

11 fus (___) dge

12 mat (___) lse

13 coa (___) imb

14 int (___) ath

15 shu (___) umb

B 10

5

Find a word that can be put in front of each of the following words to make new, compound words.

Example cast fall ward pour   *down*

16 knob   step   mat   bell   _____

17 by   still   point   pipe   _____

18 keeper   table   scale   share   _____

19 paper   agent   reel   flash   _____

20 ache   burn   beat   felt   _____

B 11

5

Find the four-letter word hidden at the end of one word and the beginning of the next word. The order of the letters may not be changed.

Example   The children had bats and balls.   *sand*

21 She is at her wits' end with her homework.   _____

22 Please empty your pockets before putting your trousers in the laundry.   _____

23 The tins are at the back of the cupboard.   _____

24 As it hurtled down the street, the car turned and spun round.   _____

25 The fiercest of dinosaurs lived throughout the cretaceous age.   _____

B 21

5

Find and underline the two words which need to change places for each sentence to make sense.

Example   She went to <u>letter</u> the <u>write</u>.

26 Who have could dreamed that it would come true?

27 After computer I like to play on my school.

28 Two plus four is two.

29 It is never steal to right.

30 Where in the China is world?

B 17

5

Give the missing numbers in the following sequences.

	Example	2	4	6	8	<u>10</u>	<u>12</u>
31	15	12	9	6	___	___	
32	11	33	___	77	___	121	
33	128	64	32	___	8	___	
34	5	8	12	17	___	___	
35	54	45	36	___	18	___	

5

Fill in the crosswords so that all the given words are included. You have been given one letter as a clue in each crossword.

36

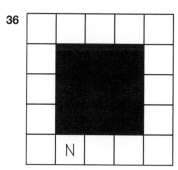

their, enter, paint, price

37

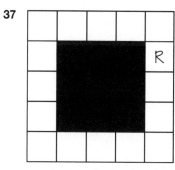

event, stand, shade, draft

38

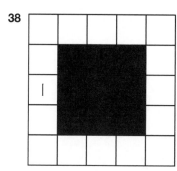

reign, thorn, faint, flair

39

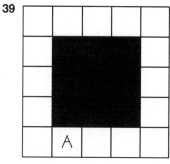

tardy, truth, taint, holly

40

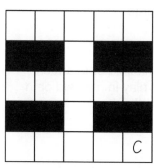

magic, flown, attic, ghost

5

Choose two words, one from each set of brackets, to complete the sentences in the best way.

B 15

Example   Smile is to happiness as (drink, <u>tear</u>, shout) is to (whisper, laugh, <u>sorrow</u>).

41 First is to last as (late, second, aged) is to (fine, young, final).

42 Shirt is to cloth as (sock, shoe, earring) is to (string, grass, leather).

43 Past is to present as (once, lessen, increase) is to (multiply, last, first).

44 Halve is to double as (change, third, force) is to (remain, second, unravel).

45 Constant is to always as (final, unique, copied) is to (original, late, related).

5

If the code for C H A N G E A B L E is written ! ' £ $ % ^ £ & * ^, what are the codes for the following words?

B 24

46 HANG   _____

47 ABLE   _____

What do these codes stand for?

48 & £ * *   _____

49 & ^ £ $ _____

50 £ ! ' ^   _____

5

Underline the one word which **cannot be made** from the letters of the word in capital letters.

B 7

Example   STATIONERY   stone   tyres   ration   <u>nation</u>   noisy

51 PORCELAIN   plain   clear   price   race   relay

52 COMMERCIAL   cream   realm   alert   moral   rice

53 GRINDSTONE   tried   stored   noted   rested   nesting

54 INVESTIGATE   tease   sting   ingest   testing   starve

55 SIGNATURE   agent   ignore   rents   great   surge

5

In football Alison can play in goal or in defence. Soraya can play in midfield or in attack. James never plays in goal, but can play in other positions. Lena can play in midfield or in attack. Kim can play in any position. Geeta can play in defence or midfield.

B 25

56 Who can play in any position except in goal?   _____

57 Which two children play the same positions?   _____

58 If Alison is ill, who will play in goal?   _____

59 How many children can play in attack? _____

60 How many children can play in midfield but not defence? _____

5

Rearrange the muddled letters in capitals to make a proper word. The answer will complete the sentence sensibly.

B 16

    Example   A BEZAR is an animal with stripes.   ZEBRA

61 We put one foot in front of the other when we LWKA. _____

62 NALIF is another word for last. _____

63 We are taught a SENLOS. _____

64 I have TPSNE all my pocket money. _____

65 Twenty-six REELTTS make up the alphabet. _____

5

Now go to the Progress Chart to record your score!   Total 65

Paper 4

Underline the two words, one from each group, which are closest in meaning.

B 3

    Example   (race, shop, <u>start</u>)   (finish, <u>begin</u>, end)

1 (push, trace, flash)   (take, shove, fly)

2 (weed, creep, weep)   (rush, cry, flip)

3 (spoil, try, mend)   (ignore, waste, repair)

4 (refuse, control, retry)   (manage, oppose, enjoy)

5 (uphold, agree, stay)   (refuse, support, change)

5

Find the three-letter word which can be added to the letters in capitals to make a new word. The new word will complete the sentence sensibly.

B 22

    Example   The cat sprang onto the MO. <u>USE</u>

6 We had chocolate PUDG for dessert. _____

7 It is a SE that it is raining, as we wanted to go out. _____

8 We had MALADE on our toast. _____

9 She decided to SPRLE marshmallows on her hot chocolate. _____

10 The store AGER asked the customers if she could help them. _____

5

Find the letter that will end the first word and start the second word.

Example peac (<u>h</u>) ome

11 mas (___) nit

12 sal (___) ach

13 tin (___) ard

14 pri (___) ask

15 man (___) dit

Find a word that can be put in front of each of the following words to make new, compound words.

Example cast   fall   ward   pour   <u>down</u>

16 doors	side	line	fit	_____
17 works	monger	clad	ware	_____
18 man	flake	drop	ball	_____
19 ball	lash	shadow	lid	_____
20 man	card	code	box	_____

Find the four-letter word hidden at the end of one word and the beginning of the next word. The order of the letters may not be changed.

Example The children had bats and balls.   <u>sand</u>

21 Each inspector must be well trained.   _____

22 The tired old man came along the street slowly.   _____

23 The *Golden Pride* approached slowly along the track.   _____

24 He had certainly made advances with his handwriting.   _____

25 He applied for his library card because he liked reading.   _____

Change the first word of the third pair in the same way as the other pairs to give a new word.

Example bind, hind   bare, hare   but, <u>hut</u>

26 pit, tip   rat, tar   tub, _____

27 made, mace   fade, face   ride, _____

28 part, start   pale, stale   peer, _____

29 seal, sale   meal, male   fear, _____

30 flea, leaf   stag, tags   plea, _____

5

5

5

5

Complete the following sentences by selecting the most sensible word from each group of words given in the brackets. Underline the words selected.

Example The (<u>children</u>, books, foxes) carried the (houses, <u>books</u>, steps) home from the (greengrocer, <u>library</u>, factory).

31 The fastest (girl, cheetah, car) in the (shop, school, forest) came (last, once, first) in the 100 metre race.

32 I wonder if we will be (calling, eating, taking) a spelling (cry, test, man) next (cake, week, word).

33 (Charging, Flying, Climbing) mountains can be (trusting, easy, dangerous) in poor (weather, hunger, air).

34 Daisy (felt, wondered, knew) whether she should (try, fall, rub) to call for (food, excellence, assistance).

35 (Always, Never, Forever) forget to (start, make, brush) your (feet, hands, teeth) before going to bed.

5

Find and underline the two words which need to change places for each sentence to make sense.

Example She went to <u>letter</u> the <u>write</u>.

36 Once upon a woman there lived an old time.

37 There been have two assemblies today.

38 The baby was crying the through all night.

39 This is the very last tell I am going to time you!

40 I wonder that he decided to do why?

5

Complete the following expressions by filling in the missing word.

Example Pen is to ink as brush is to _paint_

41 Three is to third as nine is to _____ .

42 Spain is to Spanish as France is to _____ .

43 Month is to year as decade is to _____ .

44 High is to low as up is to _____ .

45 Land is to dry as sea is to _____ .

5

Give the two missing pairs of letters and numbers in the following sequences. The alphabet has been written out to help you.

A B C D E F G H I J K L M N O P Q R S T U V W X Y Z

Example CQ DP EQ FP _GQ_ _HP_

46 C F I L __ __

47 DC DD DE DF __ __

48	A3	B5	C7	___	E11	___
49	YB	WD	___	SH	QJ	___
50	___	___	RQ	NM	JI	FE

5

Solve the problems by working out the letter codes. The alphabet has been written out to help you.

B 24

A B C D E F G H I J K L M N O P Q R S T U V W X Y Z

Example   In a code SECOND is written as UGEQPF. How would you write THIRD?   VJKTF

51 In a code PRINCE is written as NPGLAC. How would you write NICE?   _____

52 In a code ICON is written as HBNM. What does SVHF stand for?   _____

53 In a code APE is written as BRH. How would you write LOOK?   _____

54 In a code FEEL is written as IHHO. How would you write WAIT?   _____

55 In a code RICE is written as VMGI. How would you write DOG?   _____

5

Ann and Rhinffrew like lemonade. Peter likes cola, but not lemonade. Siobhan likes orange and cola. Angus only likes cola.

B 25

56 Which is the most popular drink?   _____

57 Which person likes the most types of drink?   _____

2

Chester is west of Birmingham, but east of Bangor. Shrewsbury is south of Chester.

B 25

58 Which town is furthest west?   _____

1

Three years ago Simeon was three years old. In four years' time he will be twice the age of his sister Sophie. Their mother is five times Simeon's age now. Their father is two years older than their mother.

B 25

59 How old will Sophie be in four years' time?   _____

60 How old was their mother three years ago?   _____

61 How old is their father now?   _____

62 How much older is Simeon than Sophie?   _____

4

If a = 1, b = 3, c = 4, d = 6, e = 10, find the answer to these calculations.

B 26

63 $e - d =$ _____

64 $d \div b =$ _____

65 $a + b + c =$ _____

3

Now go to the Progress Chart to record your score!   Total   65

16

Paper 5

1–5 Look at these groups of words.

H	C	G
Homes	Containers	Games

Choose the correct group for each of the words below. Write in the letter.

skipping ___   basket ___   Cluedo ___   urn ___

den ___   flat ___   cup ___   lodge ___

casket ___   snakes and ladders ___

B 1

5

Find the three-letter word which can be added to the letters in capitals to make a new word. The new word will complete the sentence sensibly.

Example   The cat sprang onto the MO.   <u>USE</u>

6 CARS are my favourite vegetables.   _____

7 The nurse put some OINTT on the wound.   _____

8 The WING machine was full of dirty clothes.   _____

9 The old lady DEDED on her carer to help her get out of bed.   _____

10 The volcano was INIVE and no longer spewed out molten lava.   _____

B 22

5

Find the letter which will end the first word and start the second word.

Example   peac (<u>h</u>) ome

11 fin   (___) oze

12 mal   (___) ive

13 poin   (___) rip

14 kis   (___) ite

15 me   (___) age

B 10

5

Write the letters of each of the following words in alphabetical order, then circle the fifth letter in each word.

16 FAMILY   _____

17 READING   _____

18 LIGHTER   _____

19 TUESDAY   _____

20 BOUNCE   _____

B 20

5

Find the four-letter word hidden at the end of one word and the beginning of the next word. The order of the letters may not be changed.

B 21

Example   The children had bats and balls.   _sand_

21 Sarah asked her brother to turn his music down.   _____

22 The teacher announced that there appeared to be
     a problem with the computers.   _____

23 The corporal ordered his troops to stand to attention.   _____

24 'Please stop interrupting!' said the teacher.   _____

25 The sofa remained in place by the door.   _____   **5**

Add one letter to the word in capital letters to make a new word. The meaning of the new word is given in the clue.

B 12

Example   PLAN   simple   _plain_

26 EVER   not at all   _____

27 STRIP   a band of colour   _____

28 CHAP   not expensive   _____

29 THOUGH   in one side and out the other   _____

30 RESTED   taken by force   _____   **5**

Complete the following sentences by selecting the most sensible word from each group of words given in the brackets. Underline the words selected.

B 14

Example   The (children, books, foxes) carried the (houses, books, steps) home
             from the (greengrocer, library, factory).

31 (Two, three, four) times (three, four, five) makes (eight, eighteen, eighty).

32 The (force, black, strong) wind blew through the (broken, pattern, fast) window.

33 In which (shirt, shop, shape) can we buy (card, painted, chocolate) (clouds, swimmers, cakes)?

34 Who (was, would, wish) like to (eat, hide, try) on their new school (uniform, canteen, hall)?

35 We were (shot, ate, flew) at by an (untidy, uneaten, unseen) (lunch, army, bedroom).   **5**

Complete the following sentences in the best way by choosing one word from each set of brackets.

B 15

Example   Tall is to (tree, short, colour) as narrow is to (thin, white, wide).

36 Shout is to (whisper, scream, noisy) as loud is to (low, quiet, cosy).

37 Hat is to (face, head, coat) as mittens is to (cat, wool, hands).

38 Government is to (rule, elect, law) as school is to (teach, classroom, pupil).

39 Red is to (food, danger, colour) as centimetre is to (weight, green, measurement).

40 Grand is to (grown, impressive, lesson) as modest is to (reduced, proud, plain).

Fill in the crosswords so that all the given words are included. You have been given one letter as a clue in each crossword.

41

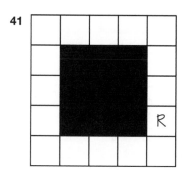

salad, daily, scale, entry

42

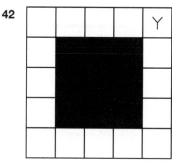

water, rings, yards, windy

43

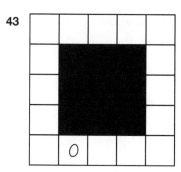

roads, elves, frame, fever

44

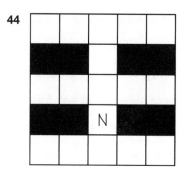

miser, sunny, funny, tryst

45

loves, caves, halls, misty

If the code for TRAVEL is USBWFM, what are the codes for the following words?

46 LEVEL   _____

47 LEAVE   _____

48 EVER   _____

If the code for CUTE is DVUF, what do these codes stand for?

49 SBSF   _____

50 MJTU   _____

If a = 3, b = 5, c = 12, d = 15, e = 2, f = 10, give the answers to these calculations as letters.

51 $d - f =$ _____

52 $a + e =$ _____

53 $b \times a =$ _____

54 $d \div a =$ _____

55 $b \times e =$ _____

Choose the word or phrase that makes each sentence true.

> **Example** A LIBRARY always has (posters, a carpet, <u>books</u>, DVDs, stairs).

56 A DESK always has (glass, books, pens, legs, children).

57 A LAKE is always (sandy, wet, salty, blue, deep).

58 A TRUCK always has (a steering wheel, four seats, passengers, petrol, carpet).

59 A COUNTRY always has (a king, a queen, a parliament, a border, a president).

60 GLASS is always (hard, transparent, clean, square, frosted).

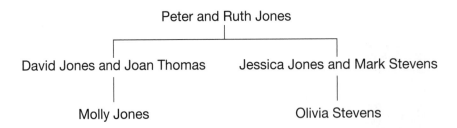

61 Peter is David's (brother, uncle, father, grandfather).

62 Jessica is Ruth's (sister, aunt, mother, daughter).

63 Molly is Ruth's (daughter, sister, mother, granddaughter).

64 Olivia is David's (daughter, niece, mother, sister).

65 Peter is Mark's (father, brother, grandfather, father-in-law).

B 24

2

B 26

5

B 14

5

B 25

5

Now go to the Progress Chart to record your score!   **Total**   65

Paper 6

Underline the pair of words most similar in meaning.

B 5

Example   come, go   <u>roams, wanders</u>   fear, fare

1 awake, asleep   gift, present   sweet, bitter

2 top, peak   warm, cool   hole, hill

3 big, small   question, answer   follow, pursue

4 please, delight   create, destroy   fall, rise

5 failure, victory   judgement, decision allow, refuse

5

Find the three-letter word which can be added to the letters in capitals to make a new word. The new word will complete the sentence sensibly.

B 22

Example   The cat sprang onto the MO.   <u>USE</u>

6 He found it difficult to SK as his mouth was so dry.   ⎯⎯⎯⎯

7 You must MULLY three by three to get 9.   ⎯⎯⎯⎯

8 SE birthday is it today?   ⎯⎯⎯⎯

9 She found the question difficult to UNDERSD.   ⎯⎯⎯⎯

10 The sisters had a DISAGREET over who should get the bed near the window.   ⎯⎯⎯⎯

5

Find the letter which will end the first word and start the second word.

B 10

Example   peac (<u>h</u>) ome

11 fligh (⎯) rip

12 pra (⎯) onder

13 flak (⎯) nd

14 ris (⎯) ite

15 bea (⎯) rial

5

Rearrange the muddled letters in capitals to make a proper word. The answer will complete the sentence sensibly.

B 16

Example   A BEZAR is an animal with stripes.   <u>ZEBRA</u>

16 The time is now a ATEQRRU past five.   ⎯⎯⎯⎯

17 He had VESRREED the car into the parking space.   ⎯⎯⎯⎯

18 I like to have some RVYAG on my mashed potatoes. _____

19 The manager named the SRELPAY for the next match. _____

20 In the drought, we were all asked to NCVROSEE water. _____

B 21

Find the four-letter word hidden at the end of one word and the beginning of the next word. The order of the letters may not be changed.

Example   The children had bats and balls.   <u>sand</u>

21 The Vikings fled overland before regrouping. _____

22 Many frozen icecaps are found north of Canada. _____

23 Each term my school tests the fire alarm to make sure it is working. _____

24 Kevin ended the conversation fairly quickly. _____

25 Tom's biggest problem was the neighbours playing loud music. _____

B 18

Change the first word of the third pair in the same way as the other pairs to give a new word.

Example   bind, hind   bare, hare   but, <u>hut</u>

26 race, rate   face, fate   place, _____

27 can, cane   trip, tripe   prim, _____

28 port, sort   pane, sane   page, _____

29 stark, shark   stone, shone   stock, _____

30 file, life   pole, lope   ride, _____

B 17

Find and underline the two words which need to change places for each sentence to make sense.

Example   She went to <u>letter</u> the <u>write</u>.

31 When go you like to would to the zoo?

32 Nature is an amazing wonder of flying.

33 Island is an Britain nation in the continent of Europe.

34 I am planning to deposit fifty bank in the pounds.

35 Gabriel found that the heat about questions were extremely difficult to do.

B 15

Choose two words, one from each set of brackets, to complete the sentences in the best way.

Example   Tall is to (tree, <u>short</u>, colour) as narrow is to (thin, white, <u>wide</u>).

36 Sugar is to (grain, sweet, bitter) as lemon is to (lime, drink, sour).

37 True is to (argument, lie, truth) as vain is to (calm, preen, vanity).

38 Salad is to (can, fork, vegetables) as trifle is to (eat, pie, fruit).

39 Tooth is to (foot, mouth, clean) as brain is to (skull, nerves, blood).

40 Still is to (calm, active, fizzy) as movement is to (fast, motion, bubbly).

Fill in the crosswords so that all the given words are included. You have been given one letter as a clue in each crossword.

41
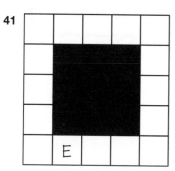

small, revel, tails, taper

42
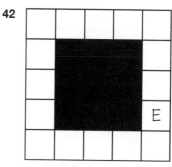

trays, place, paint, edges

43
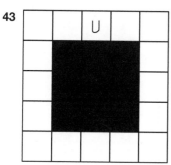

thick, falls, stick, fount

44

feeds, bride, taste, ideas

45
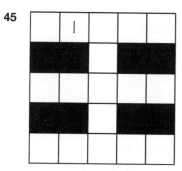

cures, moves, diver, wider

Rearrange the letters in capitals to make another word. The new word has something to do with the first two words or phrases.

Example	spot	soil	SAINT	<u>STAIN</u>
46 final	end		SALT	_____
47 prickle	bush		NORTH	_____

23

48	story	yarn	LATE	_____
49	rotten	not fresh	LEAST	_____
50	servant	hard worker	VALES	_____

5

If a = 10, b = 2, c = 3, d = 7, e = 5, give the answers to these calculations as letters.

B 26

51 $b + c + e =$ _____

52 $b \times e =$ _____

53 $a - e =$ _____

54 $(d - b) \times b =$ _____

55 $a \div b =$ _____

5

Change one word so that the sentence makes sense. Underline the word you are taking out and write your new word on the line.

B 14

Example I waited in line to buy a <u>book</u> to see the film. *ticket*

56 The train for Birmingham left the port on time. _____

57 During the freezing summer months, snow fell almost daily. _____

58 The teacher examined his patient with a stethoscope. _____

59 Queen Victoria reigned for many days in the nineteenth century. _____

60 The florist sold loaves, rolls and a selection of cakes. _____

5

Rajeev buys three magazines every week. He likes magazines about pop music, computer games and television. Carl hates football, but buys a pop music magazine. Gill buys pop music and fashion magazines. Saskia does not buy any magazines.

B 25

61 Which is the most popular magazine? _____

62 How many children buy computer game magazines? _____

2

Jan, Cilla, Vijay and Finn are friends. Finn and Vijay like gymnastics. The other children like hockey. Jan and Finn like tennis. Cilla's favourite is hockey, but she hates gymnastics. All but Finn like swimming.

B 25

63 Which is the most popular sport? _____

64 Who likes gymnastics and swimming? _____

65 Who likes three sports? _____

3

Paper 7

Underline the word in the brackets closest in meaning to the word in capitals.

Example UNHAPPY (unkind death laughter <u>sad</u> friendly)

1 TRACK (music frame scale path bed)

2 FRAIL (weak lively success timely true)

3 SOFA (table settee television bunk pillow)

4 ANTIQUE (tasty ornament fresh steady old)

5 DOMESTICATED (famous wild tamed hunted criminal)

Underline the pair of words most opposite in meaning.

Example cup, mug   coffee, milk   <u>hot, cold</u>

6 spend, save   dye, colour   fall, drop

7 fly, float   advance, retreat   clue, hint

8 soak, wet   open, full   reckless, careful

9 flexible, rigid   gentle, soft   damp, moist

10 build, support   wind, crank   clutter, order

Find the letter which will end the first word and start the second word.

Example peac (<u>h</u>) ome

11 fla   (—) ongue

12 mirro (—) ain

13 cak   (—) nter

14 ove   (—) ew

15 fur   (—) ield

Find a word that can be put in front of each of the following words to make new, compound words.

Example cast fall ward pour   <u>down</u>

16 hill   stairs   set   keep   _____

17 fall   shirt   mare   club   _____

25

18 mill	fall	melon	proof	_____
19 house	post	keeper	way	_____
20 stop	way	frame	man	_____

B 21

Find the four-letter word hidden at the end of one word and the beginning of the next word. The order of the letters may not be changed.

Example   The children had bats and balls.   *sand*

21 Please replace that book on the shelf later. _____

22 That ornament would be extremely valuable if it were not damaged. _____

23 People of my age are often asked to give advice on living a long life. _____

24 The spies watched the suspects through binoculars. _____

25 It was clear that the sack needed some urgent repair. _____

B 13

Change the first word into the last word, by changing one letter at a time and making a new, different word in the middle.

Example   CASE   *CASH*   LASH

26 FAST   _____   FACE

27 FINE   _____   FARE

28 TRAY   _____   TRIP

29 FLEW   _____   CLAW

30 BEST   _____   BEAR

B 14

Complete the following sentences by selecting the most sensible word from each group of words given in the brackets. Underline the words selected.

Example   The (children, books, foxes) carried the (houses, books, steps) home from the greengrocer, library, factory).

31 The (cow, bird, girl) sat on its (nest, chair, floor), looking after its (chicks, cubs, hands).

32 The (lazy, late, first) man on the (river, moon, sun) wore a special (spacesuit, oar, cane).

33 The (pink, young, brown) leaves fell off the (cat, trees, sky) in (autumn, spring, grass).

34 A (rabbit, friend, doctor) has to (eat, march, train) for many (meals, lungs, years).

35 The fast moving (man, river, beaver) flowed (quickly, hungrily, lazily) to the (sky, race, sea).

Find and underline the two words which need to change places for each sentence to make sense.

Example She went to <u>letter</u> the <u>write</u>.

36 You should never full with your mouth speak.

37 Can't have each we a banana?

38 Health is good for your swimming.

39 It was a very pretty day on the warm beach.

40 The old car got into his battered man.

5

Complete the following expressions by filling in the missing word.

Example Pen is to ink as brush is to *paint*

41 Box is to lid as house is to _____ .

42 Love is to hate as laugh is to _____ .

43 Tall is to taller as cool is to _____ .

44 Wales is to Welsh as Spain is to _____ .

45 Scarf is to neck as glove is to _____ .

5

Fill in the crosswords so that all the given words are included. You have been given one letter as a clue in each crossword.

46

O

house, state, match, maids

47

R

fight, flake, tiger, error

48

O

haunt, right, river, roach

49

A

sites, plait, aspen, avail

50

dress, trees, cider, tasty

5

B 26

If a = 2, b = 4, c = 6, d = 8 and e = 12, find the value of the following calculations.

51 e + b = _____

52 e − a = _____

53 a × b = _____

54 (e − d) + c = _____

55 $\dfrac{d}{b}$ = _____

5

B 16

Rearrange the letters in capitals to make another word. The new word has something to do with the first two words.

Examples spot   soil   SAINT   STAIN

56 javelin   point   REAPS   _____

57 begin   commence   TARTS   _____

58 tassle   edge   FINGER   _____

59 quiet   hushed   LISTEN   _____

60 support   love   RACE   _____

5

B 14

Choose the word or phrase that makes each sentence true.

Example   A LIBRARY always has (posters, a carpet, <u>books</u>, DVDs, stairs).

61   A SHOP always has (carpets, goods, dresses, women, stairs).

62   A BANK always has (customers, men, pictures, mirrors, money).

63   A PARTY always has (music, food, balloons, guests, gifts).

64   A GARDEN always has (flowers, a bench, trees, earth, a swing).

65   A FLORIST always has (balloons, toys, flowers, chocolates, trees).

5

1 **test, exam** Both words refer to a 'type of assessment'.
2 **rot, decay** Both words mean 'to decompose'.
3 **eat, consume** Both words mean 'to chew and swallow food'.
4 **light, pale** Both words mean 'lacking in colour and brightness'.
5 **extend, enlarge** Both words mean 'to increase in size'.
6–10 To complete this type of question, try the first word from the first set of brackets with each word in the second set of brackets. Repeat this method with the second and third words from the first set of brackets, until you find the correct combination.
6 **then, now** 'Then' is most opposite to 'now' because 'then' refers to 'the past', whereas 'now' refers to 'the present'.
7 **large, tiny** 'Large' is the most opposite to 'tiny' because 'large' means 'very big', whereas 'tiny' means 'very small'.
8 **loose, tight** 'Loose' is the most opposite to 'tight' because 'loose' means 'not held firmly or not fixed in place', whereas 'tight' means 'fixed or held firmly'.
9 **hollow, solid** 'Hollow' is the most opposite to 'solid' because 'hollow' means 'having space inside', whereas 'solid' means 'being filled inside'.
10 **first, final** 'First' is the most opposite to 'final' because 'first' means 'coming before all others' whereas 'final' means 'coming after all others'.
11–15 Try each of the words in the first set of brackets. Do they make sense with any words in the second and third set of brackets? Only one combination of three words makes sense.
11 **teacher, children, lunches**
12 **try, swimming, tide**
13 **cows, huddled, field**
14 **team, goal, match**
15 **whisked, dessert, fork**
16 **SHADES, DASHES**
17 **TEARS, RATES**
18 **PEARS, SPEAR**
19 **FLESH, SHELF**
20 **STEAL, LEAST**
21–25 For this type of question it helps to place your fingers over most of the letters, so that only four letters can be seen. Carefully work along the sentence in this way to find the hidden four-letter word. It is worth noting that the pronunciation of some letters might change.

21 **tear** He decided to have breakfas**t ear**ly that morning.
22 **carp** The garage mechanic repaired her new **car p**romptly.
23 **loan** 'Don't I get a hel**lo an**y more?' asked Mum.
24 **moon** He put a larger dyna**mo on**to the old bicycle.
25 **calm** This was a radi**cal m**ove for Professor Shirka.
26 **e** male, escape
27 **t** host, teat
28 **m** seem, made
29 **r** tear, rota
30 **p** soap, pure
31 The motor **boat** roared across the calm **lake**.
32 I thought that she couldn't hear **you**.
33 The **car** was repaired by the **mechanic**.
34 Where **do** you think she **is** going?
35 The **angry** sea roared like a **caged** lion.
36 **TU** Each letter in the first pair moves forward by two letters in the second pair.
37 **XV** Each letter in the first pair moves back by three letters in the second pair. Treat the alphabet as a loop, e.g. XYZABC etc. to work out how to move the letter A back by three.
38 **NO** Each letter in the first pair moves forward by three letters in the second pair.
39 **Z11** The letter moves forward by two and the number increases by two in the second pair.
40 **CE** The first letter in the first pair moves forward by one in the second pair. The second letter in the first pair moves forward by three in the second pair.
41 **b** bold, bread, bait, brand
42 **s** sand, sold, soup, share
43 **m** motion, may, mould, more
44 **y** your, youth, young, yell
45 **a** alive, abate, about, amend

46

S	H	A	R	K
T	■	■	■	N
A	■	■	■	E
R	■	■	■	E
T	I	L	E	S

47

F	R	O	N	T
R	■	■	■	R
E	■	■	■	I
S	■	■	■	E
H	E	A	D	S

48

A	B	O	V	E
L	■	■	■	L
O	■	■	■	V
F	■	■	■	E
T	U	F	T	S

49

R	U	P	E	E
O	■	■	■	M
U	■	■	■	P
N	■	■	■	T
D	A	I	S	Y

50

G	R	U	E	L
R	■	■	■	A
A	■	■	■	U
N	■	■	■	G
D	O	U	G	H

51–55 The easiest way to complete this type of question is to put the letters in a grid:

$	*	:	£	–	&
T	R	A	V	E	L

51 REAL is * – : &
52 TEAR is $ – : *
53 & – : £ –

@	<	?	>	!
T	R	A	I	N

54 **TAR** If @ is T, ? is A and < is R then @ ? < is TAR.
55 **TAINT** If @ is T, ? is A, > is I and ! is N then @ ? > ! @ is TAINT.
56 **tamed** There is no 'm' in 'DETAILED'.
57 **every** There is no 'y' in 'SUPERVISE'.
58 **matted** There is only one 't' in 'COMPLICATED'.
59 **games** There is no 's' in 'MANAGEMENT'.
60 **dimmer** There is only one 'm' in 'TIDEMARK'.
61 **groan** There is no 'o' in 'ESTRANGE'.

62–65

Wiston	12km	
Bridgeworth	16km	12 + 4 (distance more from London) = 12
Hanbury	22km	16 + 6 (distance more from London) = 16
Fettle	11km	22 ÷ 2 = 11 (22 is halved as fettle is half the distance than Hambury)

62 **Fettle** (11 km)
63 **Hambury** (22 km)
64 **16 km**
65 **1 km** (12 – 11)

Paper 2 (pages 5–9)

1 **build, construct** Both words mean 'to assemble'.
2 **put, place** Both words mean 'to position something'.
3 **attempt, try** Both words mean 'to make an effort'.
4 **grave, serious** Both words mean 'solemn'.

5 **easy, effortless** Both words mean 'undemanding' and 'uncomplicated'.
6 **false, true** 'False' is most opposite to 'true' because 'false' means 'contrary to fact', whereas 'true' means 'consistent with fact'.
7 **continuous, ended** 'Continuous' is most opposite to 'ended' because 'continuous' means 'going on without a break', whereas 'ended' means 'finished'.
8 **plain, elegant** 'Plain' is most opposite to 'elegant' because 'plain' means 'simple or unadorned', whereas 'elegant' means 'having style, often with adornment'.
9 **criticise, praise** 'Criticise' is most opposite to 'praise' because 'criticise' means 'to find fault with something or someone', whereas 'praise' means 'to find and state good points'.
10 **well, ill** 'Well' is most opposite to 'ill' because 'well' means 'to be in good health', whereas 'ill' means to be in 'poor health'.
11–15 Refer to Paper 1 Questions 6–10 on how to complete this type of question. It also helps to write the word combinations down for this type of question.
11 **flatmate**
12 **attack**
13 **forsake**
14 **outcry**
15 **invest**
16–17 **ROT, LOW** BRO**T**HER, FOL**LOW**ED
18–20 **MAT, ONE, ATE** CLASS**MATE**, TELEPH**ONE**, IMMEDI**ATE**LY
21–25 Refer to Paper 1 Questions 21–25 on how to complete this type of question.
21 **here** He r**e**ached the deadline in tim**e**.
22 **rope** The rusty old doo**r ope**ned with a scary creak.
23 **rare** Ta**ra re**minded her mother that Monday was a holiday.
24 **play** In winter the hen would sto**p lay**ing eggs.
25 **ease** The prisoner shouted his pl**ea se**veral times.
26–30 To complete this type of question, write the letters that have not changed into the space provided for the answer. You can then try changing each of the remaining letters to form a new word. For example:
CASE <u>AS</u> LASH
CASH must be the answer as LASE is not a word.
26 **POSH**
27 **SEAR**
28 **LOST**
29 **MINE**
30 **STAG**

31–35 Refer to Paper 1 Questions 11–15 on how to complete this type of question.

31 **arrive, holiday, resort**

32 **way, go, theatre**

33 **learner, stalling, engine**

34 **old, castle, king**

35 **mathematics, graphs, numbers**

36 **Thursday, Saturday** There is one missing day between the two.

37 **sailing, ship** 'Flight' is performed by an 'aircraft', as 'sailing' is performed by a 'ship'.

38 **shore, lake** The edge of a 'plate' is called a 'rim', as the edge of a 'lake' is called a 'shore'.

39 **restricted, unlimited** These are opposite in meaning, as are 'uncertain' and 'sure'.

40 **considerate, generous** These are synonyms, as are 'trivial' and 'insignificant'.

41 / **42**

43 / **44**

45

46–50 Look at the numbers that are next to one another in the question. They will have been either been added to, subtracted from, multiplied or divided to get to the next number in the sequence. Sometimes there may be two sequences which alternate in a question: the first, third and fifth numbers follow one sequence and the second, fourth and sixth follow another.

46 **54, 42** The number decreases by 4 each time.

47 **16, 21** The number added increases by 1 each time: +2, +3, +4, +5, +6.

48 **7, 7** The sequence alternates in the following way: +4, –2, +4, –2 etc.

49 **25, 30** The sequence alternates in the following way: +10, –5, +10, –5 etc.

50 **16, 64** Each number in the sequence is multiplied by 2.

51–55 The easiest way to complete this type of question is to put the letters in a grid:

<	>	?	?	£	%	X	£	+
B	A	L	L	I	S	T	I	C

51 BALLS is **< > ? ? %**

52 LIST is **? £ % X**

53 STAB is **% X > <**

54 ILL is **£ ? ?**

55 CALL is **+ > ? ?**

56 **drained** There is only one 'd' in 'REMAINDER'.

57 **plank** There is no 'l' in 'WORKMANSHIP'.

58 **version** There is no 'r' in 'TELEVISION'.

59 **nearest** There is no 's' in 'ARRANGEMENT'.

60 **plain** There is no 'i' in 'PERSONAL'.

61–62 A table is the easiest way to sort the information, like this:

	France	England	Wales	Scotland	Brazil
Anna	✓	✓			
Liam		✓	✓		
Malik			✓	✗	
Donna		✓		✓	✓
David	✗	✗	✗	✗	✗

61 **4**

62 **England**

63–65 Refer to Paper 1 Questions 62–65 on how to complete this type of question.

63–64 Begin with: Eleanor = 5 km, then Francesca
= 3 km (5 – 2)
Su = 1 km (5 – 4)
Robert = 2 km (1 + 1)

63 **Eleanor**

64 **2 km**

65 **Jessica and Lianne** Begin with the fact that Ellie = 10, so Jessica is 7 (10 – 3), Lily = 11 (10 + 1) Lianne is 7 (11 – 4) and Charlotte = 12 (7 + 5). Jessica and Lianne are twins as they are the only girls of the same age.

Paper 3 (pages 9–13)

1 **drag** 'Pull' and 'tug' mean 'to move something using effort' as does 'drag'.

2 **butterfly** 'Wasp' and 'beetle' are insects as is a 'butterfly'.

3 **apple** 'Pomegranate' and 'tomato' are fruit as is an 'apple'. The other choices are vegetables.

4 **agreement** 'Contract' and 'pact' are 'formal

deals'. An 'agreement' can be 'a formal or informal deal' but is closest in meaning.

5 **Russia** 'Wales' and 'Finland' are countries as is 'Russia'. The other choices are English cities or counties.

6–10 Refer to Paper 1 Questions 6–10 on how to complete this type of question.

6 **love, hate** 'Love' is the most opposite to 'hate' because 'love' is a 'strong feeling of affection', whereas 'hate' is 'a strong dislike'.

7 **hard, effortless** 'Hard' is the most opposite to 'effortless' because 'hard' means 'difficult', whereas 'effortless' means 'easy'.

8 **waste, conserve** 'Waste' is the most opposite to 'conserve' because 'waste' means 'to use carelessly', whereas 'conserve' means 'to avoid waste by using sparingly'.

9 **fair, dark** 'Fair' is the most opposite to 'dark' because 'fair' means 'light' and 'dark' means 'lacking in light or brightness'.

10 **infinite, limited** 'Infinite' is the most opposite to 'limited' because 'infinite' means 'endless', whereas 'limited' means 'restricted within certain limits'.

11 **e** fuse, edge

12 **e** mate, else

13 **l** coal, limb

14 **o** into, oath

15 **n** shun, numb

16 **door** doorknob, doorstep, doormat, doorbell

17 **stand** standby, standstill, standpoint, standpipe

18 **time** timekeeper, timetable, timescale, timeshare

19 **news** newspaper, newsagent, newsreel, newsflash

20 **heart** heartache, heartburn, heartbeat, heartfelt

21–25 Refer to Paper 1 Questions 21–25 on how to complete this type of question.

21 **send** She is at her wit**s' end** with her homework.

22 **seem** Please **em**pty your pockets before putting your trousers in the laundry.

23 **area** The tins **are a**t the back of the cupboard.

24 **cart** As it hurtled down the street, the **car t**urned and spun round.

25 **sage** The fiercest of dinosaurs lived throughout the cretaceou**s age**.

26 Who **could have** dreamed that it would come true?

27 After **school** I like to play on my **computer**.

28 Two plus **two** is **four**.

29 It is never **right** to **steal**.

30 Where in the **world** is **China**?

31–35 Refer to Paper 2 Questions 46–50 on how to complete this type of question.

31 **3, 0** Each number in the sequence decreases by 3.

32 **55, 99** Each number in the sequence increases by 22.

33 **16, 4** Each number in the sequence is divided by 2.

34 **23, 30** The number added increases by 1 each time: +3, +4, +5, +6, +7

35 **27, 9** Each number in the sequence decreases by 9.

41 **aged, young** 'First' is the opposite of 'last' as 'aged' is the opposite of 'young'.

42 **shoe, leather** A 'shirt' can be made of 'cloth' as a 'shoe' can be made of 'leather'.

43 **lessen, multiply** 'Past' is the opposite of 'present' as 'lessen' is the opposite of 'multiply'.

44 **change, remain** 'Halve' is the opposite of 'double' as 'change' is the opposite of 'remain'.

45 **unique, original** 'Constant' means the same as 'always' as 'unique' means the same as 'original'.

46–50 The easiest way to complete this type of question is to put the letters in a grid:

!	'	£	$	%	^	£	&	*	^
C	H	A	N	G	E	A	B	L	E

46 **' £ $ %** If H is ', A is £, N is $ and G is % then HANG is ' £ $ %

47 **£ & * ^** If A is £, B is &, L is * and E is ^ then ABLE is £ & * ^

48 **BALL** If & is B, £ is A and * is L then & £ * * is BALL.

49 **BEAN** If & is B, ^ is E, £ is A and $ is N then &
   ^ £ $ is BEAN.
50 **ACHE** If £ is A, ! Is C, ' is H and ^ is E then £ ! '
   ^ is ACHE.
51 **relay** There is no 'y' in 'PORCELAIN'.
52 **alert** There is no 't' in 'COMMERCIAL'.
53 **rested** There is only one 'e' in 'GRINDSTONE'.
54 **starve** There is no 'r' in 'INVESTIGATE'.
55 **ignore** There is no 'o' in 'SIGNATURE'.
56–60 A table is the easiest way to sort the
   information, like this:

	Goal	Defence	Midfield	Attack
Alison	✓	✓		
Soraya			✓	✓
James	✗	✓	✓	✓
Lena			✓	✓
Kim	✓	✓	✓	✓
Geeta		✓	✓	

56 **James**
57 **Soraya, Lena**
58 **Kim**
59 **4**
60 **2**
61 **WALK**
62 **FINAL**
63 **LESSON**
64 **SPENT**
65 **LETTERS**

Paper 4 (pages 13–16)

1–5 Refer to Paper 1 Questions 6–10 on how to
   complete this type of question.
 1 **push, shove** 'Push' and 'shove' mean 'to
   move something or someone with force'.
 2 **weep, cry** 'Weep' and 'cry' mean 'to shed
   tears'.
 3 **mend, repair** 'Mend' and 'repair' mean 'to
   restore to sound condition after damage'.
 4 **control, manage** 'Control' and 'manage'
   mean 'to exercise influence over something or
   somebody'.
 5 **uphold, support** 'Uphold' and 'support' mean
   'to prevent from falling'.
 6 **DIN** PUDDING
 7 **HAM** SHAME
 8 **ARM** MARMALADE
 9 **INK** SPRINKLE
10 **MAN** MANAGER
11 **k** mask, knit
12 **e** sale, each
13 **y** tiny, yard
14 **m** prim, mask

15 **e** mane, edit
16 **out** outdoors, outside, outline, outfit
17 **iron** ironworks, ironmonger, ironclad, ironware
18 **snow** snowman, snowflake, snowdrop,
   snowball
19 **eye** eyeball, eyelash, eyeshadow, eyelid
20 **post** postman, postcard, postcode, postbox
21–25 Refer to Paper 1 Questions 21–25 on how to
   complete this type of question.
21 **chin** Each in**sp**ector must be well trained.
22 **meal** The tired old man ca**me al**ong the street
   slowly.
23 **idea** The *Golden Pride* **a**pproached slowly
   along the track.
24 **dead** He had certainly ma**de ad**vances with
   his handwriting.
25 **heap He a**pplied for his library card because
   he liked reading.
26 **but** The first word is reversed so 'tub'
   becomes 'but'.
27 **rice** The third letter in the first word is changed
   from 'd' to 'c' so 'ride' becomes 'rice'.
28 **steer** The first letter in the first word is
   changed from 'p' to 'st' so 'peer' becomes
   'steer'.
29 **fare** The first letter remains the same; the
   second letter in the first word becomes the
   last letter in the second word; the third letter
   becomes the second letter; and the fourth
   letter becomes the third letter.
30 **leap** The first letter of the first word is moved
   to the end so 'plea' becomes 'leap'.
31–35 Refer to Paper 1 Questions 11–15 on how to
   complete this type of question.
31 **girl, school, first**
32 **taking, test, week**
33 **climbing, dangerous, weather**
34 **wondered, try, assistance**
35 **never, brush, teeth**
36 Once upon a **time** there lived an old **woman**.
37 There **have been** two assemblies today.
38 The baby was crying **all** through **the** night.
39 This is the very last **time** I am going to **tell** you!
40 I wonder **why** he decided to do **that?**
41 **ninth** 'Third' is the ordinal version of 'three' as
   'ninth' is the ordinal version of 'nine'.
42 **French** People born in 'Spain' are 'Spanish' as
   people born in 'France' are 'French'.
43 **century** A 'year' can be broken down into
   smaller time periods of 'months' as a 'century'
   can be broken down into smaller time periods
   of 'decades'.
44 **down** 'Low' is the opposite of 'high' as 'down'
   is the opposite of 'up'.
45 **wet** Without rain, land's natural state is 'dry'
   whereas the sea's natural state is 'wet'.

46 **O, R** The letters move forward by three each time.

47 **DG, DH** The first letter in each pair does not change. The second letter moves forward by one each time.

48 **D9, F13** The letter in each pair moves forward by one letter. The number increases by 2 each time.

49 **UF, OL** The first letter in each pair moves back by two letters. The second letter moves forward by two letters.

50 **ZY, VU** The first letter has moved back by four letters, as has the second letter.

51–55 The easiest way to complete this type of question is to put the example given in a grid and write how many places the letter has been moved along the alphabet. Then complete another grid and use the same rule to find out the code or letters in the answer:

S	E	C	O	N	D
+2	+2	+2	+2	+2	+2
U	G	E	Q	P	F

T	H	I	R	D
+2	+2	+2	+2	+2
V	J	K	T	F

51 **LGAC** To get from the word to the code, move each letter back two places.

52 **TWIG** To get from the code to the word, move each letter forward one place.

53 **MQRO** To get from the word to the code, move letters forward by one, then two, then three, then four places.

54 **ZDLW** To get from the word to the code, move each letter forward three places.

55 **HSK** To get from the word to the code, move each letter forward four places.

56–57 A table is the easiest way to sort the information, like this:

	Lemonade	Cola	Orange
Ann	✓		
Rhinffrew	✓		
Peter	✗	✓	
Siobhan		✓	✓
Angus	✗	✓	x

56 **cola**

57 **Siobhan**

58 **Bangor** To work this out, try drawing a diagram showing the compass points, then fill in place names:

N

W   Bangor   Chester   Birmingham   E

Shrewsbury

S

59–62 Refer to Paper 1 Questions 62–65 on how to complete this type of question. Begin by working out Simeon's age now (6). In four years time he will be 10, so Sophie will be 5. Their mother must therefore be 6 × 5, which is 30. Their father is 32 (30 + 2).

59 **5**

60 **27** (30 – 3)

61 **32**

62 **5 years** (Use ages in four years' time, i.e. 10 – 5 = 5)

63 **4** (10 – 6)

64 **2** (6 ÷ 3)

65 **8** (1 + 3 + 4)

Paper 5 (pages 17–20)

1–5 Category H contains words to do with homes (**den, flat, lodge**).
Category C contains words to do with containers (**basket, urn, cup, casket**).
Category G contains words to do with games (**skipping, Cluedo, snakes and ladders**).

6 **ROT** CAR**ROT**S

7 **MEN** OINT**MEN**T

8 **ASH** W**ASH**ING

9 **PEN** DE**PEN**DED

10 **ACT** IN**ACT**IVE

11 **d** fin**d**, **d**oze

12 **l** mal**l**, **l**ive

13 **t** poin**t**, **t**rip

14 **s** kis**s**, **s**ite

15 **w** me**w**, **w**age

16 A F I L Ⓜ Y

17 A D E G Ⓘ N R

18 E G H I Ⓛ R T

19 A D E S Ⓣ U Y

20 B C E N Ⓞ U

21–25 Refer to Paper 1 Questions 21–25 on how to complete this type of question.

21 **herb** Sarah asked **her b**rother to turn his music down.

22 **reap** The teacher announced that the**re ap**peared to be a problem with the computers.

23 **lord** The corpora**l ord**ered his troops to stand to attention.

24 **pint** 'Please stop **int**errupting!' said the teacher.

25 **fare** The so**fa re**mained in place by the door.

26 **NEVER**

A6

27 **STRIPE**

28 **CHEAP**

29 **THROUGH**

30 **WRESTED**

31–35 Refer to Paper 1 Questions 11–15 on how to complete this type of question.

31 **Two, four, eight**

32 **strong, broken**

33 **shop, chocolate, cakes**

34 **would, try, uniform**

35 **shot, unseen, army**

36 **whisper, quiet** 'Whisper' is the opposite of 'shout', as 'quiet' is the opposite of 'loud'.

37 **head, hands** A 'hat' is worn on the 'head' as, 'mittens' are worn on 'hands'.

38 **rule, teach** A 'government' is in place to 'rule', as a 'school' is in place to 'teach'.

39 **colour, measurement** 'Red' is a 'colour', as a 'centimetre' is a 'measurement'.

40 **impressive, plain** 'Grand' can mean the same as 'impressive' as 'modest' can mean the same as 'plain'.

41
S	C	A	L	E
A				N
L				T
A				R
D	A	I	L	Y

42
W	I	N	D	Y
A				A
T				R
E				D
R	I	N	G	S

43
F	R	A	M	E
E				L
V				V
E				E
R	O	A	D	S

44
M	I	S	E	R
		U		
F	U	N	N	Y
		N		
T	R	Y	S	T

45
H	A	L	L	S
		O		
C	A	V	E	S
		E		
M	I	S	T	Y

46–50 Refer to Paper 4 Questions 51–55 on how to complete this type of question. To get from the word to the code, move each letter forward one place. To get from the code to the word, move each letter back one place.

46 **MFWFM**

47 **MFBWF**

48 **FWFS**

49 **RARE**

50 **LIST**

51 **b** 15 − 10 = 5, which is b.

52 **b** 3 + 2 = 5, which is b.

53 **d** 5 × 3 = 15, which is d.

54 **b** 15 ÷ 3 = 5, which is b.

55 **f** 5 × 2 = 10, which is f

56–60 'Always' is the key word for the correct answer. Other answers may sometimes be applicable, but they will not always be true.

56 **legs**

57 **wet**

58 **a steering wheel**

59 **a border**

60 **hard**

61–65 Peter and Ruth Jones are married. They had two children: a boy called David, who married Joan Thomas and had a daughter, Molly Jones; and a girl called Jessica who married Mark Stevens and had a daughter, Olivia Stevens.

61 **father** Peter is David's father.

62 **daughter** Jessica is Ruth's daughter.

63 **granddaughter** Molly is Ruth's granddaughter.

64 **niece** Olivia is David's niece.

65 **father-in-law** Peter is Mark's father-in-law (as Jessica is Peter's daughter).

Paper 6 (pages 21–24)

1 **gift, present**

2 **top, peak**

3 **follow, pursue**

4 **please, delight**

5 **judgement, decision**

6 **PEA** SPEAK

7 **TIP** MULTIPLY

8 **WHO** WHOSE

9 **TAN** UNDERSTAND

10 **MEN** DISAGREEMENT

11 **t** flight, trip

12 **y** pray, yonder

13 **e** flake, end

14 **k** risk, kite

15 **t** beat, trial

16 **QUARTER**

17 **REVERSED**

18 **GRAVY**

19 **PLAYERS**

20 **CONSERVE**

21–25 Refer to Paper 1 Questions 21–25 on how to complete this type of question.

21 **dove** The Vikings fle**d ove**rland before regrouping.

22 **nice** Many frozen **ice**caps are found north of Canada.

23 **real** Each term my school tests the fi**re al**arm to make sure it is working.

24 **vine** Kevin ended the conversation fairly quickly.
25 **then** Tom's biggest problem was **the** neighbours playing loud music.
26 **plate** The third letter changes from 'c' to 't'.
27 **prime** 'e' is added to the end of the first word each time.
28 **sage** The first letter changes from 'p' to 's'.
29 **shock** The second letter changes from 't' to 'h'.
30 **dire** The first and third letters swap places, so 'ride' becomes 'dire'.
31 When **would** you like to **go** to the zoo?
32 **Flying** is an amazing wonder of **nature**.
33 **Britain** is an **island** nation in the continent of Europe.
34 I am planning to deposit fifty **pounds** in the **bank**.
35 Gabriel found that the **questions** about **heat** were extremely difficult to do.
36 **sweet, sour** 'Sweet' and 'sour' are opposites. Sugar is sweet and lemon is sour.
37 **truth, vanity** 'Truth' and 'vanity' are nouns related to the adjectives 'true' and 'vain'.
38 **vegetables, fruit** 'Vegetables' can be found in salad and 'fruit' can often be found in a trifle.
39 **mouth, skull** A 'tooth' is found in the 'mouth' whereas a 'brain' is found in the 'skull'.
40 **calm, motion** 'Calm' can mean 'still' and 'motion' means 'movement'.

41
T	A	I	L	S
A				M
P				A
E				L
R	E	V	E	L

42
P	L	A	C	E
A				D
I				G
N				E
T	R	A	Y	S

43
F	O	U	N	T
A				H
L				I
L				C
S	T	I	C	K

44
B	R	I	D	E
		D		
F	E	E	D	S
		A		
T	A	S	T	E

45
W	I	D	E	R
		I		
M	O	V	E	S
		E		
C	U	R	E	S

46 **LAST**
47 **THORN**
48 **TALE**

49 **STALE**
50 **SLAVE**
51 **a** $2 + 3 + 5 = 10$, which is a.
52 **a** $2 \times 5 = 10$, which is a. (When letters are placed next to one another, without a +, – × or ÷ sign between them, they need to by multiplied.)
53 **e** $10 - 5 = 5$, which is e.
54 **a** $(7 - 2) \times 2 = 5 \times 2 = 10$, which is a. This is BIDMAS (Brackets, Indices, Division, Multiplication, Addition, Subtraction). Complete the equation in the brackets first, then complete the rest of the sum.
55 **e** $10 \div 2 = 5$, which is e.
56 **port, station** The train for Birmingham left the station on time.
57 **summer, winter** During the freezing winter months, snow fell almost daily.
58 **teacher, doctor** The doctor examined his patient with a stethoscope.
59 **days, years** Queen Victoria reigned for many years in the nineteenth century.
60 **florist, baker** The baker sold loaves, rolls and a selection of cakes.
61–62 A table is the easiest way to sort out information, like this:

	Pop music	Computer games	Television	Fashion
Rajeev	✓	✓	✓	
Carl	✓			
Gill	✓			✓
Saskia	✗	✗	✗	✗

61 **Pop music**
62 **1**
63–65

	Gymnastics	Hockey	Tennis	Swimming
Jan		✓	✓	✓
Cilla	✗	✓		✓
Vijay	✓			✓
Finn	✓		✓	✗

63 **swimming**
64 **Vijay**
65 **Jan**

Paper 7 (pages 25–28)

1 **path** 'Path' is another word for 'track'.
2 **weak** 'Weak' is another word for 'frail'.
3 **settee** "Settee' is another word for 'sofa'.
4 **old** 'Old' is another word for 'antique'.
5 **tamed** 'Tamed' is another word for 'domesticated'.

6 **spend, save** 'Spend' means 'to part with money', whereas 'save' means 'to retain money'.

7 **advance, retreat** 'Advance' means 'to go forward', whereas 'retreat' means 'to go back'.

8 **reckless, careful** 'Reckless' means 'without care', whereas, 'careful' means 'with care'.

9 **flexible, rigid** 'Flexible' means 'capable of bending or changing', whereas 'rigid' means 'incapable of bending or changing'.

10 **clutter, order** 'Clutter' means a 'confused, messy state', whereas 'order' means a 'state of tidiness or neatness'.

11 **t** flat, tongue

12 **r** mirror, rain

13 **e** cake, enter

14 **n** oven, new

15 **y** fury, yield

16 **up** uphill, upstairs, upset, upkeep

17 **night** nightfall, nightshirt, nightmare, nightclub

18 **water** watermill, waterfall, watermelon, waterproof

19 **gate** gatehouse, gatepost, gatekeeper, gateway

20 **door** doorstop, doorway, doorframe, doorman

21–25 Refer to Paper 1 Questions 21–25 on how to complete this type of question.

21 **flat** Please replace that book on the shel**f lat**er.

22 **torn** That **orn**ament would be extremely valuable if it were not damaged.

23 **gear** People of my a**ge ar**e often asked to give advice on living a long life.

24 **swat** The spie**s wat**ched the suspects through binoculars.

25 **knee** It was clear that the sac**k nee**ded some urgent repair.

26–30 Refer to Paper 2 Questions 26–30 on how to complete this type of question.

26 **FACT**

27 **FIRE**

28 **TRAP**

29 **FLAW**

30 **BEAT**

31–35 Refer to Paper 1 Questions 11–15 on how to complete this type of question.

31 **bird, nest, chicks**

32 **first, moon, spacesuit**

33 **brown, trees, autumn**

34 **doctor, train, years**

35 **river, quickly, sea**

36 You should never **speak** with your mouth **full**.

37 Can't **we** each **have** a banana?

38 **Swimming** is good for your **health**.

39 It was a very **warm** day on the **pretty** beach.

40 The old **man** got into his battered **car**.

41 **roof** A box has a 'lid' on it and a house has a 'roof' on it.

42 **cry** 'Love' is the opposite of 'hate' and 'laugh' is the opposite of 'cry'.

43 **cooler** 'Taller' means 'more tall' and 'cooler' means 'more cool'.

44 **Spanish** People from 'Wales' are 'Welsh' and people from 'Spain' are 'Spanish'.

45 **hand** A 'scarf' is worn round the 'neck' and a 'glove' is worn on the 'hand'.

46  47

48 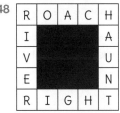 49

50

51 **16** 12 + 4 = 16

52 **10** 12 − 2 = 10

53 **8** 2 × 4 = 8

54 **10** (12 − 8) + 6 = 4 + 6 = 10 This is BIDMAS: (brackets, indices, division, multiplication, addition and subtraction) complete the equation in the brackets first, then complete the rest of the sum.

55 **2**

56 **SPEAR**

57 **START**

58 **FRINGE**

59 **SILENT**

60 **CARE**

61–65 'Always' is the key word for the correct answer. Other answers may sometimes be applicable, but they will not always be true.

61 **goods**

62 **money**

63 **guests**

64 **earth**

65 **flowers**

EXPANDED ANSWERS

1–5 Category A contains musical instruments
(**violin, guitar, piano, flute**).
Category B contains parts of speech (**noun,
verb, preposition**).
Category C contains computer terms (**monitor,
hard drive, mouse**)

6 **pull, push** 'Pull' means to 'move something
towards you', whereas 'push' means to 'move
something away from you'.

7 **wild, tame** 'Wild' means 'untamed', whereas
'tame' means 'domesticated'.

8 **shut, open** 'Shut' means 'closed', whereas
'open' means 'not closed'.

9 **combine, separate** 'Combine' means 'join
together', whereas 'separate' means 'take
apart'.

10 **friend, enemy** A 'friend' is someone who can
be can trusted, whereas an 'enemy' cannot as
they are an opponent.

11 **s** dress, sign

12 **y** play, yoke

13 **l** shall, love

14 **t** trait, tiara

15 **l** drill, long

16–20 Refer to Paper 1 Questions 6–10 on how to
complete this type of question. It also helps to
write the word combinations down for this type
of question.

16 **takeaway**

17 **update**

18 **blameless**

19 **office**

20 **peanut**

21–25 Refer to Paper 1 Questions 21–25 on how to
complete this type of question.

21 **wasp** Joe **was p**leased he didn't have any
homework that night.

22 **bush** He was surprised when the **bus h**alted at
the stop.

23 **thin** Janine felt proud of herself for finishing
four**th in** the race.

24 **seat** Apples **eat**en quickly will give you
indigestion.

25 **army** The c**ar my** brother just bought is bright
red.

26–30 Refer to Paper 2 Questions 26–30 on how to
complete this type of question.

26 **RICE**

27 **MEAT**

28 **PLAY**

29 **FLAT**

30 **BEAR**

31 **O15** The letter in each pair moves forward by two
letters. The number in each pair increases by 2.

32 **YW** Both letters move back by three letters.
The alphabet should be considered a
continuous loop, e.g XYZABCD etc.

33 **FI** Both letters move forward by five letters.

34 **PD** The first letter in each pair moves forward
by six letters, and the second letter moves
back by six letters.

35 **MO** Both letters move forward by four letters.

36

T	R	U	S	T
A				H
M				O
E				S
S	H	O	V	E

37

P	R	I	Z	E
R				V
E				E
S				R
S	U	N	N	Y

38

I	C	I	N	G
N				R
P				A
U				V
T	A	N	G	Y

39

U	L	T	R	A
		Y		
H	A	P	P	Y
		E		
H	A	S	T	Y

40

F	U	N	N	Y
		I		
R	I	G	H	T
		H		
T	I	T	L	E

41 **sort** 'Sort' can mean 'kind' or 'type' as well as
to 'select' or 'choose'.

42 **play** 'Play' can mean 'frolic' or 'romp' as well
as a 'performance' or 'drama'

43 **fly** 'Fly' is a type of 'insect' or 'bug' and is also
associated with 'travel' or 'aeroplane'.

44 **stab** 'Stab' can mean an 'attempt' or 'try' as
well as 'knife' or 'jab'.

45 **kid** 'Kid' is associated with 'child' and 'young',
but also means to 'tease' or 'fool'.

46–50 Refer to Paper 1 Questions 51–55 on how to
complete this type of question.

46 **TIE** If 7 = T, 3 = I M = 4 and 5 = E then 735 =
TIE

47 **MAT** If 2 = T, 8 = A, 3 = M and 9 = E then
382 = MAT

48 **RED** If 4 = D, 3 = E and 7 = R then 734 = RED

49 **LEAP** If 6 = P, 9 = E, 1 = A and 3 = L then
3916 = LEAP

50 **TALE** if 4 = L, 3 = A, 2 = T and 1 = E then
2341 = TALE

51–53 Refer to Paper 1 Questions 62–65 on how to
complete this type of question.

Begin with: blue scored 20 points. Next red scored 10 points (half of blue score). Next yellow scored 15 (10 + 5). Finally green scored 12 (20 – 8).

51 **blue team**
52 **15**
53 **10**
54 **Tuesday** Tuesday was two days ago, so today is Thursday. In five days' time it will be Tuesday again.
55 **14** David is now 19 (23 – 4), so five years ago he was 14 (19 – 5).
56 **e** 2 + 8 = 10, which is e.
57 **b** 12 – 8 = 4, which is b.
58 **c** 2 × 4 = 8, which is c.
59 **f** 2 + 4 + 6 = 12, which is f.
60 **b** 8 ÷ 2 =, which is b.
61 **EGILMNT**
62 **T**
63 **G**
64 **ARSTY**
65 **S**

Paper 9 (pages 32–36)

1 **bread**
2 **right**
3 **bold**
4 **scream**
5 **amazed**
6 **sad** 'Joyful' means 'happy', so 'sad', which means 'unhappy', is the most opposite.
7 **raise** 'Lower' means 'to move further down', so 'raise', which means 'to move up', is the most opposite.
8 **arrive** 'Leave' means 'to go away', so 'arrive', which means 'to get to your destination', is the most opposite.
9 **exclude** 'Include' means 'to consider as part of', so 'exclude', which means 'to leave out', is the most opposite.
10 **join** 'Separate' means 'to move apart', so 'join', which means 'to link together', is the most opposite.
11 **RUM TRUMPETS**
12 **RAN RESTAURANT**
13 **OWN CROWNS**
14 **ARM HARMONY**
15 **TEA TEACHER**
16–20 Refer to Paper 1 Questions 6–10 on how to complete this type of question. It also helps to write the word combinations down for this type of question.
16 **undertake**
17 **upright**
18 **throughout**

19 **downstairs**
20 **cupboard**
21–25 Refer to Paper 1 Questions 21–25 on how to complete this type of question.
21 **then** We will be the next group to get a table.
22 **bite** Kate's rabbit enjoys munching on lettuce and carrots.
23 **send** Our holiday to Mauritius ended on a Saturday.
24 **pout** It is difficult to skip outside in the long grass.
25 **mask** My mum asked everyone to be quiet because the baby was sleeping.
26 **I** fit, flame
27 **s** word, tolls
28 **s** mile, self
29 **f** able, scarf
30 **e** rob, event
31–35 Refer to Paper 1 Questions 11–15 on how to complete this type of question.
31 **goalkeeper, save, match**
32 **eat, vegetables, good**
33 **old, walk, stick**
34 **dress, modern, belt**
35 **time, ancient, witch**
36 **huge, short** 'Huge' is the opposite of 'tiny' in the same way as 'short' is the opposite of 'long'.
37 **early, excited** 'Early' is the opposite of 'late' in the same way as 'excited' is the opposite of 'calm'.
38 **crowded, bare** 'Crowded' is similar in meaning to 'full' in the same way as 'bare' is similar in meaning to 'empty'.
39 **fasten, twist** 'Fasten' is similar in meaning to 'tie' in the same way as 'twist' is similar in meaning to 'turn'.
40 **rest, stay** 'Rest' is similar in meaning to 'pause' in the same way as 'stay' is similar in meaning to 'remain'.

41

Q	U	I	L	L
U				A
E				R
E				G
R	A	N	G	E

42

F	L	O	O	R
R				H
I				Y
E				M
D	R	A	P	E

43

C	R	E	P	E
H				R
E				A
E				S
R	I	F	L	E

44

G	R	A	V	E
		F		
M	I	T	R	E
		E		
F	I	R	E	S

45

B	I	T	E	S
		R		
T	H	A	N	K
		P		
T	A	S	T	E

46 **PK, PM** The first letter does not change. The second letter moves forward by two letters.

47 **M, S** The letter moves forward by three letters each time.

48 **Q9, O11** The letter moves back by two letters each time. The number increases by 2 each time.

49 **OJ, RH** The first letter in each pair moves forward by three letters. The second letter moves back by two letters.

50 **KM, PH** The first letter in the pair moves on by one letter, then two letters, then three letters, etc. The second letter in the pair moves back by one letter, then two letters, then three letters, etc.

51–55 First look for letters that appear once only and match their position. 'O' occurs once and is second position so must be represented by '8', which occurs once. 'I' occurs once and is in third position, so must be represented by '4'. 'R' appears last twice, and once first, so must be represented by '7'. 'T' appears as last letter twice and second last letter twice so must be '2'. 'P' appears twice as first letter, so must be represented by '1'. 'A' appears second twice and third once, so is represented by '3'. This leaves 'S', which is represented by '5'. These can then best be shown as a simple chart":

O	I	R	T	P	A	S
8	4	7	2	1	3	5

51 **7325**

52 **5237**

53 **5247**

54 **1352**

55 **1852**

56 **ACJKOPST**

57 **T**

58 **K**

59 **CNORTUY**

60 **T**

61–62 Refer to Paper 1 Questions 62–65 on how to complete this type of question.
Begin with the fact that Jem is 5. Jim must be 7 (5 + 2). Jam is 10 (7 + 3).

61 **Jem**

62 **10**

63–65 A table is the easiest way to sort out information, like this:

	English	German	Spanish	Italian
Jean	✓	✓	✓	
Malek		✓	✓	✓
Geeta	✓	✓	✓	
Martin		✓	✓	✓
Sophie		✓		✓

63 **English**

64 **German**

65 **Italian**

Paper 10 (pages 37–40)

1 **sponge, ship** The other three words are bodies of water.

2 **twig, nest** The other three words are types of bird.

3 **heart, friend** The other three words are synonyms meaning to worship or respect.

4 **next, future** The other three words are adjectives meaning 'of great age'.

5 **undecided, complicated** The other three words are nouns meaning the final part of something.

6 **INK DRINK**

7 **TEN EATEN**

8 **PAR COMPARE**

9 **LIT POLITE**

10 **OUR COLOUR**

11 **rot**

12 **dice**

13 **deal**

14 **bear**

15 **treat**

16–20 Refer to Paper 1 Questions 21–25 on how to complete this type of question.

16 **bare** Mum replied that Jake and Cale**b are**n't playing today.

17 **torn** The zoo's alliga**tor n**ever came out of the pool except for food.

18 **fear** In those days a ser**f ear**ned his living with great difficulty.

19 **hall** It is important to catc**h all** shots coming in his direction.

20 **arch** The star **ch**anged shape when looked at through the telescope.

21 **p** late, cramp

22 **e** prim, gape

23 **t** tile, sight

24 **r** stand, brought

25 **c** mine, clay

26 **lunch**

27 **sly**

28 **knock**

29 **poke**

30 **green**

31–35 Refer to Paper 1 Questions 11–15 on how to complete this type of question.

31 **horse, hay, stable**

32 **night, hooting, distance**

33 **road, ways, traffic**

34 **teacher, pupils, homework**

35 **girls, mother, cinema**

36 It was too **rainy** to play **outside**.

37 The last **day** of the **year** is a Sunday.

38 January is the **first month** of the year.

39 Did you have **lasagne** for your **lunch?**

40 The **baby** was crying until her **mother** gave her a dummy.

41 **LN** Each letter in the first pair moves back by one letter in the second pair.

42 **S19** The letter in the first pair moves forward by two letters. The number in the first pair increases by 2 in the second pair.

43 **OP** Each letter in the first pair moves forward by four letters in the second pair.

44 **WU** This is a 'mirror' pattern: imagine a mirror line between 'M' and 'N' in the alphabet. A and C are the first and third letters of the alphabet, whilst Z and X are the last and third to last. D and F are the fourth and sixth letters of the alphabet, so W and U are the fourth to last and sixth to last letters of the alphabet.

45 **TV** Each letter in the first pair moves forwards by nine letters in the second pair.

46–50 Refer to Paper 1 Questions 6–10 on how to complete this type of question.

46 **quick, slow** 'Quick' is most opposite to 'slow' because 'quick' means to 'move at a fast speed', whereas 'slow' means to 'move at a low speed'.

47 **save, spend** 'Save' is most opposite to 'spend' because 'save' means to 'hold onto money', whereas 'spend' means to 'part with it'.

48 **attack, retreat** 'Attack' is most opposite to 'retreat' because 'attack' means to 'launch an assault', whereas 'retreat' means to 'withdraw from an assault'.

49 **near, distant** 'Near' is most opposite to 'distant' because 'near' means 'close by' and 'distant' means 'far away'.

50 **specific, general** 'Specific' is most opposite to 'general' because 'specific' means precise and clear, whereas 'general' means imprecise and approximate.

51–55 **citsilaer, taerter, tcane, tcarter, tsomla**
Written backwards the words are: tcarter, taerter, tsomla, tcane, citsilaer. Write the words

into a grid and put them in alphabetical order by looking at each column in turn:

T	C	A	R	T	E	R			
T	A	E	R	T	E	R			
T	S	O	M	L	A				
T	C	A	N	E					
C	I	T	S	I	L	A	E	R	

56–60 Refer to Paper 1 Questions 51–55 on how to complete this type of question.

56–58 **612, 9123, 9136** If S = 3, T = 6, I = 1, L = 9 and E = 2, then TIE = 612, LIES = 9123 and LIST = 9136.

59–60 **SURE, HUES** If R = 3, U = 4, S = 5, H = 7 and E = 2, then 5432 = SURE and 7425 = HUES.

61–62 A table is the easiest way to sort out information, like this:

	Sweets	Toffee	Chocolate	Fudge
Ann	✓	✓	✗	
Jean			✓	✓
Beata	✓		✓	✗
Gosia	✓		✓	

61 **toffee and fudge**

62 **chocolate and sweets**

63–65 A table is the easiest way to sort out information, like this:

	First	Second	Third	Fourth	Fifth	Sixth
Mohammed	✓	✗	✗	✗	✗	✗
Ann	✗	✗	✓	✗	✗	✗
Eric	✗	✗	✗			✓
Charlotte	✗	✗	✗		✓	✗
Bob	✗		✗	✓		✗
Farooq	✗	✓	✗		✗	✗

63 **Eric**

64 **Ann**

65 **Farook**

Paper 11 (pages 40–44)

1 **cheerful, happy**

2 **disappear, vanish**

3 **flash, flare**

4 **career, profession**

5 **pay, salary**

6 **ROW** NARROW

7 **RAW** STRAWBERRIES

8 **KIN** BIKINI

9 **SIT** HESITATE

10 **TAR** NECTARINES

Bond Verbal Reasoning Assessment Papers 9–10 years Book 2

11 **house** housework, houseboat, housekeeper, household

12 **sea** seashell, seashore, seaside, seasick

13 **down** downstairs, downpour, downhill, downbeat

14 **back** backstage, backbone, backfire, backstroke

15 **watch** watchtower, watchdog, watchword, watchmaker

16–20 Refer to Paper 1 Questions 21–25 on how to complete this type of question.

16 **hate** She somehow managed to lose her **hat** **e**very week.

17 **ants** The baby eleph**ant s**at down rather clumsily.

18 **sour** We made the decoration**s our**selves.

19 **slay** The tiny kitten**s lay** peacefully on the rug.

20 **rope** My dad complained because I left the fridge doo**r ope**n.

21–25 Refer to Paper 2 Questions 26–30 on how to complete this type of question.

21 **GALE**

22 **POST** or **PART**

23 **BEST**

24 **CREW**

25 **SPAR**

26 The **music** on the **radio** was very relaxing.

27 We finally **managed** to **reach** the bus stop.

28 His birthday was on the last **day** of the **month**.

29 The old **lions** were too tired to go **hunting**.

30 Why are we having to **wait** in this long **queue**?

31

32

33

34

35

36 **AK, AM** The first letter in each pair remains the same. The second letter moves forward by two letters.

37 **OS, RV** Each letter in the pair moves forward by three letters.

38 **LI, NK** Each letter in the pair moves forward by two letters.

39 **DQ, DO** The first letter in each pair follows the sequence B, B, C, C, D, D. The second letter moves back by two letters.

40 **IR, HS** The first letter in each pair moves back by one letter. The second letter moves forward by one letter.

41–45 Refer to Paper 1 Questions 51–55 on how to complete this type of question.

▲	♥	◆	○	•	♥	&
T	E	A	C	H	E	R

41 ◆ ○ • ♥

42 & ♥ ◆ ○ •

43 ○ • ♥ ◆ ▲

44 **HEAR**

45 **RATE**

46–47 **Eagles eat mice. Eagles are predators.** Eagles hunt small creatures and mice are small creatures, so this is true. An animal is a predator if it hunts other creatures for food, so this is also true.

48–49 **Spain is hot. Palm trees never grow in cold countries.** One statement says that palm trees only grow in hot countries and the other says that they are grown in Spain, so Spain must be a hot country. Also, as palm trees only grow in hot countries they must never grow in cold countries.

50–51 **Earth is further from the Sun than Venus. Venus is hotter than Earth.** As Mars is not mentioned in the opening statements, we can discount the two options that include Mars. No indication is given about the relative positions of Mercury and Earth, so this can be discounted too. This leaves just two answers that must be true.

52–53 A table is the easiest way to sort out information, like this:

	Coronation Street	Emmerdale	Eastenders
Ewan	✓		✓
Joaquin			✓
Alice	✓	✓	
Gemma		✓	✓

52 *Eastenders*

53 **Joaquin**

54–55 A table is the easiest way to sort out information, like this:

	Laptop	Television	Smart Speaker
Rashid	✓	✗	✓
Peta	✗	✓	✗
Molly	✓	✓	✓
Annie	✗	✓	✓
Tom	✓	✗	✓

54 **Molly**

55 **Rashid and Tom**

56 **t** 4 + 6 = 10, which is t.

57 **q** 12 − 8 = 4, which is q.

58 **s** 2 × 4 = 8, which is s.

59 **r** 12 ÷ 2 = 6, which is r.

60 **u** 2 × (12 − 6) = 2 × 6 = 12, which is u. This is BIDMAS. Complete the equation in the brackets first, then complete the rest of the sum.

61–65 Refer to Paper 4 Questions 51–55 on how to complete this type of question.

61 **PCKN** To get from the word to the code, move each letter forward two places.

62 **QDRS** To get from the word to the code, move each letter back one place.

63 **GOOD** To get from the code to the word, move each letter back one place.

64 **BSX** To get from the word to the code, move the first and third letters back one place, and move the second and fourth letters forward one place.

65 **QLRDE** To get from the word to the code, move each letter back three places.

Paper 12 (pages 45–48)

1 **smart, fast** The other three words are concerned with size.

2 **body, smile** The other three words are names of body parts.

3 **mud, sand** The other three words are names of tree species.

4 **desert, ocean** The other three words are names of channels of flowing water.

5 **field, meadow** The other three words are concerned with movement.

6 **PEN** SHAR**PEN**

7 **PIP** HOSE**PIPE**

8 **ADD** **ADD**ITION

9 **EAR** S**EAR**CH

10 **APE** P**APER**

11 **y** every, yellow; happy, yule

12 **r** faster, ruby; miser, route

13 **t** fright, terror; spat, table

14 **r** rear, rise; pair, round

15 **l** foul, light; call, load

16–20 Refer to Paper 1 Questions 6–10 on how to complete this type of question. It also helps to write the word combinations down for this type of question.

16 **netball**

17 **flatmate**

18 **pattern**

19 **goodwill**

20 **manage**

21–25 Refer to Paper 1 Questions 21–25 on how to complete this type of question.

21 **hiss** The king finished **his s**peech by wishing everyone goodnight.

22 **mane** The old **man e**njoyed seeing his grandchildren.

23 **pear** The Po**pe ar**rived back at the Vatican late that night.

24 **tilt** They sat under the umbrella and talked un**til t**he sun went down.

25 **vein** Clodagh was very bra**ve in** the hospital.

26 **h** self, shell

27 **n** brow, shone

28 **s** hare, smash

29 **c** rate, pact

30 **e** last, tone

31 When the wind blows, the **leaves** fall from the **trees**.

32 He thought that he had come **first** in the **race**.

33 Please eat your **breakfast** and clear away your **bowl**.

34 The winner won a **gold** medal and the runner-up a **silver** one.

35 You have to **dig** deep to **find** the hidden treasure.

36 **HX** Each letter in the first pair moves forward by two letters in the second pair.

37 **QN** Each letter in the first pair moves back by three letters in the second pair.

38 **WM** The first letter in the pair moves forward by four letters. The second letter moves back by four letters.

39 **WD** The first letter in the pair does not change. The second letter moves forward by one letter.

40 **JQ** The first letter in the pair moves back by one letter. The second letter moves forward by one letter.

41–45 'N' appears twice in 'NINE' so must be 2528. 'I' must therefore be 5 and 'E' must be 8. Three words begin with 'P' which must therefore be 3. You can now work out the codes for 'NINE' and 'PINE'. There only one code that begins '28' (NE) so 2849 = NEAR: therefore A = 4 and R = 9. That leaves 1 = T.

N	I	E	P	A	R	T
2	5	8	3	4	9	1

41 **3491**

42 **3428**

43 **3528**

44 **2849**

45 **2528**

46–48 A table is the easiest way to sort out information, like this:

	Goldfish	Hamster	Cat	Dog	Mouse
Danny			✓	✓	
Ella			✓	✓	
Petra	✓	✓			
Li		✗	✓	✓	✓
Sharif				✓	

46 **Li**

47 **cat and dog**

48 **Sharif**

49 **2** 10 − 5 = 5 (Annabelle's age now); 5 − 3 = 2 (Annabelle's age three years ago).

50 **5** 12 + 2 = 14 (Jamie's sister's age in two years' time); 14 ÷ 2 = 7 (Jamie's age in two year's time); 7 − 2 = 5 (Jamie's age now).

51 **H** 2 + 2 + 2 = 6, which is H.

52 **H** 12 − 6 = 6, which is H.

53 **F** 2 × 2 = 4, which is F.

54 **D** 24 ÷ 12 = 2, which is D.

55 **H** 2 × (6 ÷ 2) = 2 × 3 = 6, which is H. This is BIDMAS. Complete the equation in the brackets first, then complete the rest of the sum.

56 **flower, petrol** I went to the petrol station to fill up my car for the long journey.

57 **garage, vet** Ellen took her sick hamster to the vet.

58 **moon's, sun's** The cat liked to sleep near the window to catch the last of the sun's rays.

59 **foot, neck** The swan stretched its graceful, long neck as it floated in the pond.

60 **marshmallow, cream** My favourite sort of ice cream is chocolate.

61–65 Refer to Paper 4 Questions 51–55 on how to complete this type of question.

61 **UDWHV** To get from the word to the code, move each letter forward three places.

62 **RNWO** To get from the word to the code, move letter forward two places.

63 **SALE** To get from the code to the word, move the first letter back one place; move the second letter back two places; move the third letter back three places, etc.

64 **SHOW** This is an alternating sequence. To get from the code to the word, move the first and third letters back two places; move the second and fourth letters forward two places.

65 **PDVN** To get from the word to the code, move each letter forward three places.

Paper 13 (pages 48–52)

1 **B** (fruits)

2 **D** (vegetables)

3 **C** (drinks)

4 **A** (meats)

5 **B** (fruits)

6–10 Refer to Paper 1 Questions 6–10 on how to complete this type of question.

6 **hunt, search** Both words mean 'to look for'.

7 **similar, alike** Both words mean 'having a resemblance'.

8 **overtake, pass** Both words mean 'to go past'.

9 **show, display** Both words mean 'to present to view'.

10 **vague, unclear** Both words mean 'not clear'.

11 **pass** 'Pass' is the opposite of 'fail' which means to 'not pass' (in an exam context, for example).

12 **conflict** 'Conflict' can refer to a war, which is the opposite of 'peace'.

13 **damage** 'Damage', which means 'to cause destruction', is the opposite of 'repair' which means 'to put damage right'.

14 **follow** 'Follow', which means 'to go after' is the opposite of 'lead', which means 'to go ahead of' or 'to go in front of'.

15 **doubtful** 'Doubtful', which means 'unsure' is the opposite of 'certain', which means 'without doubt'.

16 **can** A 'can' is a container, as are 'pot' and 'tin'; if you 'can' do something it means you are 'willing' or 'able'.

17 **light** 'Light' can mean 'delicate' or 'weightless' as well as 'to ignite' or 'to flare'.

18 **hit** 'Hit' can mean to 'smack' or 'strike' as well as a 'success' or 'chart-topper'.

19 **bright** 'Bright' can mean 'light' or 'shining' as well as 'able' or 'clever'.

20 **smart** 'Smart' can mean 'elegant' or 'stylish' as well as 'hurt' or 'ache'.

21 **green** greenhouse, greenfly, greengrocer, greenfinch

22 **wood** woodpecker, woodworm, woodcutter, woodwind

23 **fire** fireplace, firearm, firefighter, fireside

24 **hand** handbag, handshake, handrail, handwriting
25 **hair** hairbrush, haircut, hairband, hairdresser
26–30 Refer to Paper 1 Questions 21–25 on how to complete this type of question.
26 **sand** All the boy**s and** girls played sensibly at break-time.
27 **lace** Alex was ready for his grand ga**la ce**ntenary celebrations.
28 **torn** The famous ac**tor n**ever once forgot her lines.
29 **term** Af**ter m**y hard work, I was glad to have scored top in my class.
30 **fort** I usually read **for t**hirty minutes before I go to bed.
31 **man**
32 **sore**
33 **plot**
34 **hop**
35 **rip**
36 We put the cake in the **oven** to **bake**.
37 We put the names in alphabetical order so **Annabel** came before **Bindy**.
38 I sometimes count on my **fingers** when doing my maths **homework**.
39 The **wild** rose is often white or **red** in colour.
40 I have **read** seven pages of my **red** level book.
41 **e** stare, earth
42 **h** crash, hall
43 **r** hair, rail
44 **t** pact, tear
45 **k** elk, knew
46–50 F must be 8 as it is the only first letter to appear once. Thus 'FALL' is 8277, so A = 2 and L = 7. This means 'TOOL' is 5117, so T = 5 and O = 1. 'BOOT' must be 3115, so B = 3. BAIL must be 3297, so I = 9.

F	A	L	T	O	B	I
8	2	7	5	1	3	9

46 **3115**
47 **8277**
48 **2751**
49 **5117**
50 **3297**
51–52 If David is not beside Asif, Peter must be in the middle. Asif is on the right, so David is on the left.
51 **David**
52 **Peter**
53 **16** In six years' time Alice's sister will be 8, so Alice will be 8 × 2 which is 16.
54 **23** Robert is now 9 (4 + 5). In five years' time he will be 14 (9 + 5), so his brother will be 28 (2 × 14). His brother is now 23 (28 – 5).

55 **Town D** The towns are best shown as a diagram, like this:

	B	C
D	A	F

56 **PAIRS**
57 **EXITS**
58 **SAUCE**
59 **SAGE**
60 **DANGER**
61 **butcher, baker** The baker had baked several cakes.
62 **Tame, Wild** Wild animals do not make very good pets.
63 **hole, nest** The bird had constructed a beautiful nest out of twigs.
64 **Sunday, December** December is the last month of the calendar year.
65 **nurse, teacher** The teacher asked her pupils to take their seats.

Paper 14 (pages 52–55)

1 **swift, fast** Both words mean 'quick'.
2 **back, rear** Both words mean 'the hindmost part of something'.
3 **miniature, small** Both words mean 'tiny'.
4 **aim, goal** Both words refer to a 'target'.
5 **pole, rod** Both words refer to a 'straight bar'.
6 **brilliant, dull** 'Brilliant' means 'very bright' and is the opposite of 'dull', which means 'lacking brightness'.
7 **rude, polite** 'Rude' means 'ill-mannered' and is the opposite of 'polite', which means 'well-mannered'.
8 **rise, fall** 'Rise' means 'to move up' and is the opposite of 'fall', which means to 'move down'.
9 **criticise, praise** 'Criticise' means 'to find fault with' and is the opposite of 'praise', which means 'to find good points'.
10 **relaxed, tense** 'Relaxed' means 'free from tension and anxiety' and is the opposite of 'tense' which means 'highly strung' and 'not relaxed at all'.
11 **plain** 'Plain' can mean 'obvious' or 'apparent'; it can also refer to 'fields' or 'grassland'.
12 **grace** 'Grace' can mean 'elegance' or 'beauty'; it can also refer to 'a type of prayer' or 'thanks'(especially for food).
13 **pack** 'Pack' can mean 'to fill or arrange' (as with luggage or shopping); it can also refer to a 'bundle' or 'parcel'.
14 **grain** 'Grain' can mean 'a particle or speck'; it can also refer to 'cereals' and 'seeds'.

Bond Verbal Reasoning Assessment Papers 9–10 years Book 2

15 **star** 'Star' can be linked with the sun and sky; it is also a colloquial word that can refer to a 'celebrity' or 'actor'.

16 **e** stare, ever; mane, entry

17 **t** cart, tangy; hint, tumble

18 **d** sad, dame; hod, drink

19 **k** plank, kill; hunk, knit

20 **p** soup, pale; ramp, prove

21–25 Refer to Paper 1 Questions 21–25 on how to complete this type of question.

21 **hole** Who le**t** the cat in?

22 **edge** My dad's she**d ge**nerally is rather messy.

23 **cane** Tremors from a severe earthquake **can e**nd up many miles away.

24 **this** Fraser lent Sam a pencil because he'd left **his** at home.

25 **rind** I understand that aspi**rin d**eadens pain in the back.

26–30 Refer to Paper 2 Questions 26–30 on how to complete this type of question.

26 **PART**

27 **MIST**

28 **SOAR**

29 **BRAT**

30 **CUTS**

31–35 The easiest way to complete this type of question is to put the letters in a grid and write in how the position number of the letters has changed. Sometimes there are two letters the same in the words given, so both of these need to be tried before finding a real word.

31 **TEST**

1		2	3	4		1		2	3	4	
P	A	L	E		S	T	I	R	T	A	K	E	S	T	O	P

32 **ALSO**

3	1	2		4			3	1	2		4		
S	O	A	R	T	I	M	E	S	A	L	E	O	N	L	Y

33 **PEAR**

	2		1			3	4		2		1			3	4
F	O	O	L	M	A	S	T	L	E	A	P	S	T	A	R

34 **PINT**

	1		4		2		3		1		4		2		3
P	R	I	C	E	P	A	N	I	C	S	P	E	L	T	B	I	S	O	N

35 **RARE**

	3	4			1	2			3	4			1	2	
S	T	E	A	M	C	L	E	A	R	T	R	E	N	D	C	R	E	A	M

36 **r** career, rent

37 **e** fire, edge

38 **t** cart, there

39 **t** feet, track

40 **b** lamb, barrel

41–45 Refer to Paper 1 Questions 6–10 on how to complete this type of question.

41 **pound, beat** Both words mean 'to hit with fists or an implement'.

42 **lower, reduce** Both words mean 'to lessen or make smaller'.

43 **injure, damage** Both words mean 'to cause harm'.

44 **sickness, illness** Both words mean 'poor health'.

45 **tough, strong** Both words mean 'resilient'.

46 **war** warlock, warfare, warlord, warpath

47 **water** waterfowl, waterfront, waterlogged, watercourse

48 **weather** weatherproof, weatherboard, weatherman, weathervane

49 **pass** Passover, passbook, passport, password

50 **back** backache, backspace, background, backpack

51 **QN, UN** The first letter in each pair moves forward by four letters; the second letter in each pair repeats, moves forward by one letter, then repeats again: LL, MM, NN.

52 **CC, XX** There are two sequences which alternate. In the first sequence (first, third and fifth pairs), the letters move forward by one

letter from the beginning of the alphabet. In the second sequence (second, fourth and sixth pairs) the letters move back by one letter from the end of the alphabet.

53 **RP, PN** Each letter in the first pair moves back by two letters.

54 **PO, PQ** The first letter in each pair repeats, moves forward by one letter, then repeats again: NN, OO, PP. The second letter move forward by two letters then back by one letter, repeating the sequence: +2, −1, +2, −1, +2.

55 **I5, K6** The letter in each pair moves forward by two letters; the number increases by 1.

56–60 Refer to Paper 1 Questions 51–55 on how to complete this type of question. The easiest way to complete this type of question is to put the letters in a grid:

←	↑	→	↓	↔	Υ	↑
R	E	P	L	A	C	E

56 →↑↔ ← is PEAR.
57 Υ↓↔ → is CLAP.
58 →↔ ↓↑ is PALE.
59 ↓↑↑← is LEER.
60 →↔ ↓↔Υ↑ is PALACE.

61 **wake, sleep** Mrs Stokes found that a glass of warm milk helped her sleep at night.

62 **notes, strings** One of Roger's guitar strings broke as he practised.

63 **alive, dead** After being fatally wounded, the soldier was pronounced dead when he reached the hospital.

64 **moon, sun** Watching the sun rise is a wonderful way to start the morning.

65 **hungry, full** I was so full because I ate all of my dinner and then had a second helping.

Paper 15 (pages 55–59)

1–10 Refer to Paper 1 Questions 6–10 on how to complete this type of question.

1 **ask, request** Both words mean 'to express a desire for something'.

2 **shiny, glistening** Both words describe something that is reflecting light.

3 **destroyed, broken** Both words mean 'made unusable'.

4 **cross, angry** Both words mean 'annoyed'.

5 **drum, tap** Both words mean 'to strike an object, often rhythmically'.

6 **shy, confident** 'Shy' is the most opposite of 'confident' because 'shy' means 'lacking in confidence' whereas 'confident' means 'self-assured'.

7 **cause, effect** 'Cause' is the most opposite to 'effect' because 'cause' is 'the reason for something happening' whereas 'effect' is the 'outcome'.

8 **light, heavy** 'Light' is the most opposite to 'heavy' because 'light' means 'lacking in weight' whereas 'heavy' means 'having a good deal of weight'.

9 **tired, energetic** 'Tired' is the most opposite to 'energetic' because 'tired' means 'lacking in energy' whereas 'energetic' means 'full of energy'.

10 **rare, common** 'Rare' is the most opposite to 'common' because 'rare' means 'not often found' whereas 'common' means 'often found'.

11 **r** pair, rule
12 **b** fib, base
13 **l** tool, last
14 **r** cover, rain
15 **y** puny, young

16–20 Refer to Paper 1 Questions 21–25 on how to complete this type of question.

16 **lone** You are lucky as it is the final **one** in the shop.

17 **shun** He considered the ca**sh un**necessary in the circumstances.

18 **cast** The In**cas t**aught us many interesting things.

19 **itch** The crowd qu**it ch**eering when the team lost the ball.

20 **heat** He **ate** the bag of sweets himself.

21 **b** break, brand, ball, boat
22 **c** coat, cool, clean, chain
23 **t** take, torn, toad, turn
24 **f** fir, fate, find, fault
25 **w** wind, west, would, white
26 **dragon**
27 **cove**
28 **ration**
29 **shin**
30 **meter**

31 The old **train** chugged along the endless **track**.

32 **Kent** is one of the largest counties in **England**.

33 I really enjoy classical **music** and black and white **films**.

34 It was very **late** so I ran briskly **home**.

35 The **newspaper** was delivered to the wrong **house** by mistake.

36 **slow, high** 'Slow' is opposite to 'speedy' as 'high' is opposite to 'low'.

37 **overlook, honour** 'Overlook' is similar in meaning to 'ignore' as 'honour' is similar in meaning to 'praise'.

38 **water, coal** 'Water' is found in a 'well' as 'coal' is found in a 'mine'.

39 **wet, cold** 'Wet' is similar in meaning to 'damp' as 'cold' is similar in meaning to 'cool'.

40 **bird, mammal** A 'kite' is a 'bird' as a 'badger' is a 'mammal'.

41 **10** $4 + 1 + 5 = 10$

42 **45** $20 + 10 + 10 + 5 = 45$

43 **E** $20 - 10 = 10$, which is E.

44 **E** $(1 + 4) + 5 = 5 + 5 = 10$, which is E. This is BIDMAS. Complete the equation in the brackets first, then complete the rest of the sum.

45 **D** $10 - 5 = 5$, which is D.

46 **m** claim, most; calm, men

47 **y** pray, yolk; try, young

48 **e** pace, end; craze, ease

49 **d** bald, dose; food, deck

50 **l** full, loot; scrawl, land

51 **LEAP**

52 **FALSE**

53 **WEAK**

54 **ANGERS**

55 **MELON**

56–60 Refer to Paper 2 Questions 26–30 on how to complete this type of question.

56 **PAST**

57 **MACE** or **MITE**

58 **ARMS**

59 **SNIP**

60 **FLAW**

61 **EO** Each letter in the first pair moves back by two letters.

62 **WW** This is a 'mirror' pattern: imagine a mirror line between 'M' and 'N' in the alphabet. Each pair is the same distance from the beginning and end of the alphabet, so BB and YY are second from the beginning and end. DD is fourth from the beginning; fourth from the end is WW.

63 **ST** The first letter in the pair moves forward by two letters; the second letter moves forward by three letters.

64 **ZV** The first letter in the pair is unchanged. The second letter moves back by one letter.

65 **Z26** Each letter is followed by its numerical position in the alphabet, so A1 is to B2 as Y25 is to Z26.

Paper 8

B 1

Look at these groups of words.

A	B	C
Musical instruments	Parts of speech	Computer terms

1–5 Choose the correct group for each of the words below. Write in the letter.

noun ___   monitor ___   verb ___   violin ___   hard drive ___

mouse ___   guitar ___   preposition ___   piano ___   flute ___

5

Underline the pair of words most opposite in meaning.

B 9

    Example   cup, mug   coffee, milk   <u>hot, cold</u>

  6 start, begin   pull, push   fight, battle

  7 wild, tame   medium, middle   stale, old

  8 shut, open   tight, cramped   fix, mend

  9 try, attempt   combine, separate stay, remain

10 filter, flow   friend, enemy   bump, knock

5

Find the letter that will end the first word and start the second word.

B 10

    Example   peac (<u>h</u>) ome

11 dres (___) ign

12 pla (___) oke

13 shal (___) ove

14 trai (___) iara

15 dril (___) ong

5

Underline the two words, one from each group, that go together to form a new word. The word in the first group always comes first.

B 8

    Example   (hand, <u>green</u>, for)   (light, <u>house</u>, sure)

16 (take, bring, seat)   (home, away, back)

17 (up, in, at)   (day, week, date)

18 (hunt, weak, blame)   (on, less, full)

19 (on, off, down)   (rest, step, ice)

20 (snap, pea, spice)   (nut, bag, hot)

5

Find the four-letter word hidden at the end of one word and the beginning of the next word. The order of the letters may not be changed.

B 21

Example The children had bats and balls. <u>sand</u>

21 Joe was pleased he didn't have any homework that night. _____

22 He was surprised when the bus halted at the stop. _____

23 Janine felt proud of herself for finishing fourth in the race. _____

24 Apples eaten quickly will give you indigestion. _____

25 The car my brother just bought is bright red. _____

⬭ 5

Change the first word into the last word, by changing one letter at a time and making a new, different word in the middle.

B 13

Example CASE *CASH* LASH

26 NICE _____ RACE

27 SEAT _____ MOAT

28 PLAN _____ SLAY

29 FEAT _____ FLAY

30 BEAN _____ TEAR

⬭ 5

Fill in the missing letters and numbers. The alphabet has been written out to help you.

B 23

A B C D E F G H I J K L M N O P Q R S T U V W X Y Z

Example AB is to CD as PQ is to <u>RS</u>.

31 C3 is to E5 as M13 is to _____.

32 WU is to TR as BZ is to _____.

33 HK is to MP as AD is to _____.

34 RR is to XL as JJ is to _____.

35 AC is to EG as IK is to _____.

⬭ 5

Fill in the crosswords so that all the given words are included. You have been given one letter as a clue in each crossword.

B 19

36

37

those, trust, tames, shove

press, prize, every, sunny

30

38

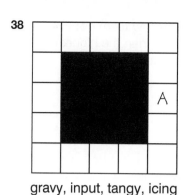

gravy, input, tangy, icing

39

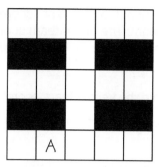

types, ultra, hasty, happy

40

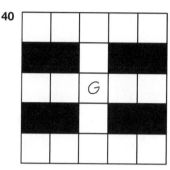

right, title, funny, night

5

B 5

Underline the one word in brackets which will go equally well with both pairs of words outside the brackets.

 Example rush, attack   cost, fee   (price, hasten, strike, <u>charge</u>, money)

41 kind, type   select, choose   (sort, gentle, take, pass, soft)

42 frolic, romp   performance, drama   (joy, act, jump, play, game)

43 insect, bug   travel, aeroplane   (fly, ant, hear, floor, listen)

44 attempt, try   knife, jab   (go, sword, stab, stake, point)

45 child, young   tease, fool   (kid, trick, badger, fox, tail)

5

B 24

46 If 7345 stands for TIME, 735 stands for _____ .

47 If 2839 stands for TAME, 382 stands for _____ .

48 If 4337 stands for DEER, 734 stands for _____ .

49 If 6913 stands for PEAL, 3916 stands for _____ .

50 If 4321 stands for LATE, 2341 stands for _____ .

5

In a class athletics competition, the blue team scored 20 points. The yellow team got five points more than the red team. The green team scored eight points less than the highest of these teams. The red team scored half as many points as the blue team.

51 Which team came top? _____

52 How many points did the yellow team score? _____

53 How many points did the red team score? _____

54 If it was Tuesday two days ago, what day will it be in five days' time? _____

55 If David will be 23 in four years' time, how old was he five years ago? _____

5

If a = 2, b = 4, c = 8, d = 6, e = 10 and f = 12, give the answers to these calculations as letters.

56 a + c = ___

57 f − c = ___

58 a × b = ___

59 a + b + d = ___

60 c ÷ a = ___

5

Answer these questions. The alphabet has been written out to help you.

A B C D E F G H I J K L M N O P Q R S T U V W X Y Z

61 Put the letters in MELTING in alphabetical order. _____

62 Which is now the last letter? _____

63 Which is now the second letter? _____

64 Put the letters in TRAYS in alphabetical order. _____

65 Which is now the third letter? _____

5

Now go to the Progress Chart to record your score! Total 65

Paper 9

Find a word that is similar in meaning to the word in capital letters and that rhymes with the second word.

Example CABLE tyre *wire*

1 LOAF head _____

2 CORRECT flight _____

3 BRAVE	hold	_____
4 SHOUT	dream	_____
5 SURPRISED	glazed	_____

5

Underline the one word in the brackets which is most opposite in meaning to the word in capitals.

B 6

Example WIDE (broad vague long <u>narrow</u> motorway)

6 JOYFUL	(old	rich	cheerful	sad	rested)
7 LOWER	(drop	raise	down	deep	below)
8 LEAVE	(behind	right	arrive	go	exit)
9 INCLUDE	(accept	exclude	add	remain	contain)
10 SEPARATE	(shrink	reduce	divide	apart	join)

5

Find the three-letter word which can be added to the letters in capitals to make a new word. The new word will complete the sentence sensibly.

B 22

Example The cat sprang onto the MO. <u>USE</u>

11 The musicians enjoyed playing their TPETS loudly. _____

12 The food was very good at the Italian RESTAUT. _____

13 The museum contained many royal CRS and robes. _____

14 The choir was singing in perfect HONY. _____

15 The swimming CHER asked the students to dive into the pool. _____

5

Underline two words, one from each group, that go together to form a new word. The word in the first group always comes first.

B 8

Example (hand, <u>green</u>, for) (light, <u>house</u>, sure)

16 (under, side, on)	(take, put, out)
17 (to, where, up)	(good, right, may)
18 (at, through, in)	(out, last, fire)
19 (side, down, on)	(stairs, case, ladder)
20 (glass, drink, cup)	(board, set, light)

5

Find the four-letter word hidden at the end of one word and the beginning of the next word. The order of the letters may not be changed.

B 21

Example The children had bats and balls. *sand*

21 We will be the next group to get a table. _____

22 Kate's rabbit enjoys munching on lettuce and carrots. _____

23 Our holiday to Mauritius ended on a Saturday. _____

24 It is difficult to skip outside in the long grass. _____

25 My mum asked everyone to be quiet because the baby was sleeping. _____

5

Move one letter from the first word and add it to the second word to make two new words.

B 13

> **Example**   hunt   sip   _hut_   _snip_

26 flit   fame   _____   _____

27 sword   toll   _____   _____

28 smile   elf   _____   _____

29 fable   scar   _____   _____

30 robe   vent   _____   _____

5

Complete the following sentences by selecting the most sensible word from each group of words given in the brackets. Underline the words selected.

B 14

> **Example**   The (children, books, foxes) carried the (houses, books, steps) home from the (greengrocer, library, factory).

31 The (score, goalkeeper, spectator) made a wonderful (save, fall, trick) to make sure we won the (treat, match, race).

32 (Eat, wash, dry) up your (water, vegetables, shoes) because they are (late, old, good) for you.

33 He was very (late, hungry, old) and found it hard to (dive, eat, walk) without a (dish, stick, paper).

34 Her (foot, dress, head) was very (modern, flat, wet) and had a wide (belt, eye, pot) on it.

35 Once upon a (day, year, time) in an (empty, ancient, easy) cottage there lived an old (witch, apple, child).

5

Choose two words, one from each set of brackets, to complete the sentences in the best way.

B 15

> **Example**   Tall is to (tree, short, colour) as narrow is to (thin, white, wide).

36 Tiny is to (wild, small, huge) as long is to (last, little, short).

37 Late is to (first, early, behind) as calm is to (excited, easy, afraid).

38 Full is to (none, crowded, alone) as empty is to (bare, last, food).

39 Tie is to (shirt, bump, fasten) as turn is to (twist, knob, first).

40 Pause is to (continue, rest, worry) as remain is to (stay, important, leftover).

5

Fill in the crosswords so that all the given words are included. You have been given one letter as a clue in each crossword.

41

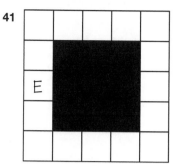

large, queer, range, quill

42

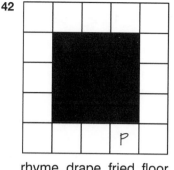

rhyme, drape, fried, floor

43

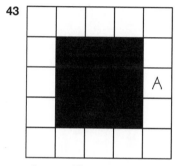

cheer, rifle, crepe, erase

44

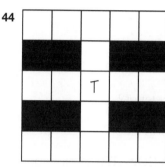

fires, after, mitre, grave

45

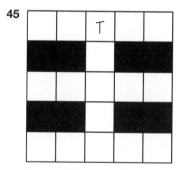

thank, bites, taste, traps

Give the two missing pairs of letters and numbers in the following sequences. The alphabet has been written out to help you.

A B C D E F G H I J K L M N O P Q R S T U V W X Y Z

	Example	CQ	DP	EQ	FP	*GQ*	*HP*
46		PC	PE	PG	PI	___	___
47		D	G	J	___	P	___
48		Y1	W3	U5	S7	___	___
49		CR	FP	IN	LL	___	___
50		AW	BV	DT	GQ	___	___

35

Here are the number codes for five words. Match the right word to the right code.

PAST	STAR	RATS	STIR	POST
5237	7325	1352	1852	5247

51 RATS _____

52 STAR _____

53 STIR _____

54 PAST _____

55 POST _____

5

56 Arrange the letters in JACKPOTS in alphabetical order. _____

57 Which is now the last letter? _____

58 Which is now the fourth letter? _____

59 Arrange the letters in COUNTRY in alphabetical order. _____

60 Which is now the fifth letter? _____

5

Three little cats are called Jim, Jam and Jem. Jim is three years younger than Jam, but is two years older than Jem, who is five.

61 Who is the youngest? _____

62 How old is Jam? _____

2

Jean, Malek, Geeta, Martin and Sophie are students. Jean and Geeta speak English, German and Spanish. Sophie speaks Italian and German. Martin and Malek speak German, Italian and Spanish.

63 Which language is spoken by the fewest children? _____

64 Which language is spoken by the most children? _____

65 Which language is spoken by three children? _____

3

Now go to the Progress Chart to record your score! Total 65

Paper 10

Underline the two words which are the odd ones out in the following groups of words.

B 4

Example   black   <u>king</u>   purple   green   <u>house</u>

1 sponge   lake   ship   sea   ocean

2 crow   pigeon   twig   nest   eagle

3 love   heart   adore   friend   admire

4 next   aged   future   elderly   old

5 undecided   complicated   conclusion   termination end

5

Find the three-letter word which can be added to the letters in capitals to make a new word. The new word will complete the sentence sensibly.

B 22

Example   The cat sprang onto the MO.   <u>USE</u>

6 Please DR up your juice.

7 The meal lay half EA on the table.

8 I think that you should COME the two options.

9 Being POE is just good manners.

10 I went to the paint shop with my Dad to decide which COL I wanted to paint my room.

5

Underline the one word which **can be made** from the letters of the word in capital letters.

B 7

Example   CHAMPION   camping   notch   peach   cramp   <u>chimp</u>

11 CONTROL   rot   cannot   call   roll   room

12 DECISION   slide   diesel   noisy   dice   scent

13 SLANDEROUS   gland   race   deal   slate   ended

14 INTOLERABLE   stale   strain   stable   bear   blame

15 ALLITERATION   creation   terrain   alight   terrapin   treat

5

Find the four-letter word hidden at the end of one word and the beginning of the next word. The order of the letters may not be changed.

B 21

Example   The children had bats and balls.   <u>sand</u>

16 Mum replied that Jake and Caleb aren't playing today.

17 The zoo's alligator never came out of the pool except for food.

37

18 In those days a serf earned his living with great difficulty. _____

19 It is important to catch all shots coming in his direction. _____

20 The star changed shape when looked at through the telescope. _____

5

Move one letter from the first word and add it to the second word to make two new words.

B 13

Example   hunt   sip   <u>hut</u>   <u>snip</u>

21 plate   cram   _____   _____

22 prime   gap   _____   _____

23 title   sigh   _____   _____

24 strand   bought   _____   _____

25 mince   lay   _____   _____

5

Find a word that is similar in meaning to the word in capital letters and that rhymes with the second word.

B 5

Example   CABLE   tyre   <u>wire</u>

26 MEAL   crunch   _____

27 CRAFTY   fly   _____

28 STRIKE   clock   _____

29 JAB   croak   _____

30 COLOUR   bean   _____

5

Complete the following sentences by selecting the most sensible word from each group of words given in the brackets. Underline the words selected.

B 14

Example   The (<u>children</u>, books, foxes) carried the (houses, <u>books</u>, steps) home from the (greengrocer, <u>library</u>, factory).

31 The (girl, ship, horse) was eating (water, hay, cable) in its (stable, current, bathroom).

32 Later that (week, day, night) an owl was heard (laughing, hooting, walking) in the (distance, flowers, table).

33 Before crossing the (river, road, sky) please look both (rafts, ways, eyes) and listen for (music, traffic, clouds).

34 The (manager, major, teacher) asked his (horses, customers, pupils) to hand in their (homework, teas, umbrellas).

35 The (girls, waiters, dentists) stood in line while their (mayor, mother, mechanic) bought tickets to the (cinema, wedding, party).

5

Find and underline the two words which need to change places for each sentence to make sense.

B 17

Example She went to <u>letter</u> the <u>write</u>.

36 It was too outside to play rainy.

37 The last year of the day is a Sunday.

38 January is the month first of the year.

39 Did you have lunch for your lasagne?

40 The mother was crying until her baby gave her a dummy.

5

Fill in the missing letters and numbers. The alphabet has been written out to help you.

B 23

A B C D E F G H I J K L M N O P Q R S T U V W X Y Z

Example AB is to CD as PQ is to <u>RS</u>.

41 TV is to SU as MO is to _____.

42 F6 is to H8 as Q17 is to _____.

43 AB is to EF as KL is to _____.

44 AC is to ZX as DF is to _____.

45 HJ is to QS as KM is to _____.

5

Underline the two words, one from each group, which are the most opposite in meaning.

B 9

Example (dawn, <u>early</u>, wake) (<u>late</u>, stop, sunrise)

46 (quick, lazy, late)   (fast, slow, busy)

47 (change, hunt, save)   (spend, follow, lie)

48 (attempt, attack, attend)   (hold, try, retreat)

49 (far, near, away)   (distant, right, move)

50 (single, different, specific)   (alone, general, unusual)

5

51–55 Write each word backwards and list them in alphabetical order.

B 20

retract   retreat   almost   enact   realistic

_____   _____   _____   _____   _____

5

If the code for STILE is 36192, what are the codes for the following words?

B 24

56 TIE   _____

57 LIES   _____

58 LIST   _____

3

If the code for RUSHES is 345725, what do the following codes stand for?

B 24

59 5432 _____

60 7425 _____

2

Ann likes sweets and toffee but not chocolate. Her sister, Jean, loves chocolate and fudge. Her friend Beata also likes chocolate and sweets, but hates fudge. Her sister Gosia likes chocolate and sweets.

B 25

61 Which two items are least popular? _____

62 Which two items are most popular? _____

2

Six children are lining up for the cinema. Mohammad is at the front and Ann is third in line. Eric does not stand next to Mohammad or Farook. Charlotte stands between Bob and Eric. Bob and Farook are not at the back of the line.

B 25

63 Who is last in line? _____

64 Who is between Farook and Bob? _____

65 Who is second in line? _____

3

Now go to the Progress Chart to record your score! **Total** **65**

Paper 11

Underline the two words in each line which are most similar in type or meaning.

B 5

	Example	<u>dear</u>	pleasant	poor	extravagant	<u>expensive</u>
1	hungry	cheerful	sad	happy		wasteful
2	display	disappear	vanish	wonder		follow
3	flash	thunder	flare	burn		fall
4	sleep	eat	career	make		profession
5	pay	loss	deposit	consideration		salary

5

Find the three-letter word which can be added to the letters in capitals to make a new word. The new word will complete the sentence sensibly.

Example The cat sprang onto the MO. <u>USE</u>

6 The lane was too NAR for a car. _____

7 My favourite fruit is STBERRIES. _____

8 A two-piece bathing suit is called a BII. _____

9 Do not HEATE to call if you need further advice. _____

10 I prefer NECINES to peaches. _____

5

Find a word that can be put in front of each of the following words to make a new, compound word.

Example cast fall ward pour <u>down</u>

11 work boat keeper hold _____

12 shell shore side sick _____

13 stairs pour hill beat _____

14 stage bone fire stroke _____

15 tower dog word maker _____

5

Find the four-letter word hidden at the end of one word and the beginning of the next word. The order of the letters may not be changed.

Example The children had bats and balls. <u>sand</u>

16 She somehow managed to lose her hat every week. _____

17 The baby elephant sat down rather clumsily. _____

18 We made the decorations ourselves. _____

19 The tiny kittens lay peacefully on the rug. _____

20 My dad complained because I left the fridge door open. _____

5

Change the first word into the last word, by changing one letter at a time and making a new, different word in the middle.

Example CASE <u>CASH</u> LASH

21 GALA _____ GATE

22 PAST _____ PORT

23 NEST _____ BENT

24 CHEW _____ BREW

25 STAR _____ SPAT

5

41

Find and underline the two words which need to change places for each sentence to make sense.

Example   She went to <u>letter</u> the <u>write</u>.

26 The radio on the music was very relaxing.

27 We finally reach to managed the bus stop.

28 His birthday was on the last month of the day.

29 The old hunting were too tired to go lions.

30 Why are we having to queue in this long wait?

Fill in the crosswords so that all the given words are included. You have been given one letter as a clue in each crossword.

31
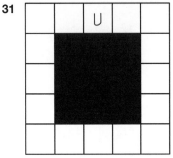

place, sleep, stunt, these

32
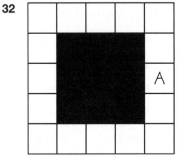

frown, names, slays, feels

33
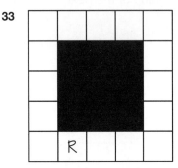

ended, freed, chose, chief

34
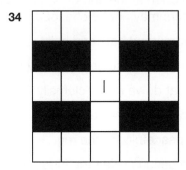

seven, prism, haste, veils

35
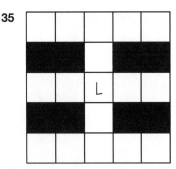

might, mists, poles, gales

Give the two missing pairs of letters in the following sequences. The alphabet has been written out to help you.

B 23

A B C D E F G H I J K L M N O P Q R S T U V W X Y Z

Example CQ   DP   EQ   FP   *GQ*   *HP*

36 AC   AE   AG   AI   ___   ___

37 CG   FJ   IM   LP   ___   ___

38 DA   FC   HE   JG   ___   ___

39 BY   BW   CU   CS   ___   ___

40 MN   LO   KP   JQ   ___   ___

5

If the code for T E A C H E R is ▲ ♥ ♦ ○ • ♥ &. What are the codes for the following words?

B 24

41 ACHE   _____

42 REACH   _____

43 CHEAT   _____

What do these codes stand for?

44 • ♥ ♦ &   _____

45 & ♦ ▲ ♥   _____

5

46–47 Read the first statement and then underline two of the five options below that must be true.

B 25

'Eagles hunt small creatures for food.'

Eagles are wild.

Eagles eat mice.

Eagles cannot see well.

People hate eagles.

Eagles are predators.

2

48–49 Read the first two statements and then underline two of the five options below that must be true.

B 25

Palm trees only grow in hot countries. Palm trees are grown in Spain.

Spain is hot.

Palm trees are found in Ireland.

Palm trees never grow in cold countries.

Spain is a city.

Palm trees grow in Antarctica.

Read the first two statements and then underline two of the five options below that must be true.

B 25

'Mercury and Venus are planets. They are closer to the Sun than Earth.'

      Earth is hotter than Mars.

      Earth is further from the Sun than Venus.

      Mars is hotter than Venus.

      Mercury and Earth are next to each other.

      Venus is hotter than Earth.

2

Ewan, Joaquin, Alice and Gemma were discussing their favourite soap operas. Ewan and Alice are the only ones who like *Coronation Street*. Only Gemma and Alice like *Emmerdale*. Joaquin, Ewan and Gemma like *Eastenders*.

B 25

52 Which is the most popular programme? _____

53 Who likes the fewest programmes? _____

2

Rashid, Peta, Molly, Annie and Tom were discussing whether they have a laptop, a television or a smart speaker in their bedroom. Only Peta and Annie did not have a laptop. Peta only had a television. Only Rashid and Tom did not have a television. Four children had a smart speaker.

B 25

54 Who had a laptop and television? _____

55 Who had all the same items? _____

2

If p = 2, q = 4, r = 6, s = 8, t = 10 and u = 12, give the answer to these calculations as letters.

B 26

56 q + r = _____

57 u − s = _____

58 p × q = _____

59 u ÷ p = _____

60 p × (u − r) = _____

5

Solve the problems by working out the letter codes. The alphabet has been written out to help you.

B 24

A B C D E F G H I J K L M N O P Q R S T U V W X Y Z

61 In a code, FINAL is written as HKPCN. What is the code for NAIL? _____

62 In a code, BROWN is written as AQNVM. How would you write REST? _____

63 In a code, MILK is written as NJML. What does HPPE stand for? _____

64 In a code, BACK is written as ABBL. How would you write CRY? _____

65 In a code, PRESS is written as MOBPP. How would you write TOUGH? _____

5

Now go to the Progress Chart to record your score!   **Total** **65**

Paper 12

Underline the two words which are the odd ones out in the following groups of words.

Example black <u>king</u> purple green <u>house</u>

1 long   wide   smart   short   fast

2 head   ankle   body   leg   smile

3 oak   mud   sand   beech   elm

4 river   desert   stream   brook   ocean

5 catch   field   haul   meadow   drag

Find the three-letter word which can be added to the letters in capitals to make a new word. The new word will complete the sentence sensibly.

Example The cat sprang onto the MO. <u>USE</u>

6 Please SHAR your pencil.   _____

7 The lack of rain has caused a HOSEE ban.   _____

8 We do ITION and subtraction in maths.   _____

9 I had to SCH my room this morning when I
couldn't find my homework.   _____

10 The teacher asked the pupils to take out some PR and a pen. _____

Find the letter which will complete both pairs of words, ending the first word and starting the second. The same letter must be used for both pairs of words.

Example mea (<u>t</u>) able   fi (<u>t</u>) ub

11 ever (___) ellow   happ (___) ule

12 faste (___) uby   mise (___) oute

13 frigh (___) error   spa (___) able

14 rea (___) ise   pai (___) ound

15 fou (___) ight   cal (___) oad

Underline two words, one from each group, that go together to form a new word. The word in the first group always comes first.

Example (hand, <u>green</u>, for)   (light, <u>house</u>, sure)

16 (net, side, hat)   (ball, case, mug)

17 (flat, hard, big)   (room, age, mate)

18 (hit, tap, pat) (ten, tear, tern)

19 (poor, open, good) (can, door, will)

20 (car, fan, man) (ate, ear, age)

5

Find the four-letter word hidden at the end of one word and the beginning of the next word. The order of the letters may not be changed.

B 21

> **Example**   The children had bats and balls.   <u>sand</u>

21 The king finished his speech by wishing everyone goodnight.   —————

22 The old man enjoyed seeing his grandchildren.   —————

23 The Pope arrived back at the Vatican late that night.   —————

24 They sat under the umbrella and talked until the sun went down.   —————

25 Clodagh was very brave in the hospital.   —————

5

Move one letter from the first word and add it to the second word to make two new words.

B 13

> **Example**   hunt   sip   <u>hut</u>   <u>snip</u>

26 shelf   sell   —————   —————

27 brown   shoe   —————   —————

28 share   mash   —————   —————

29 crate   pat   —————   —————

30 least   ton   —————   —————

5

Find and underline the two words which need to change places for each sentence to make sense.

B 17

> **Example**   She went to <u>letter</u> the <u>write</u>.

31 When the wind blows, the trees fall from the leaves.

32 He thought that he had come race in the first.

33 Please eat your bowl and clear away your breakfast.

34 The winner won a silver medal and the runner-up a gold one.

35 You have to find deep to dig the hidden treasure.

5

Fill in the missing letters. The alphabet has been written out to help you.

A B C D E F G H I J K L M N O P Q R S T U V W X Y Z

Example AB is to CD as PQ is to R̲S̲.

36 BR is to DT as FV is to _____.

37 XU is to UR as TQ is to _____.

38 PN is to TJ is to SQ is to _____.

39 WA is to WB is to WC is to _____.

40 MN is to LO as KP is to _____.

B 23

5

Here are the number codes for five words. Match the right word to the right code.

PART	PANE	NEAR	PINE	NINE
2849	2528	3528	3491	3428

41 PART _____

42 PANE _____

43 PINE _____

44 NEAR _____

45 NINE _____

B 24

5

Five children: Danny, Ella, Petra, Li and Sharif have pets. Petra has a goldfish and a hamster. Ella, Danny and Li have cats. Sharif, Li, Danny and Ella have dogs. Li does not like hamsters, but has a mouse.

46 Who has the most pets? _____

47 Which pets does Danny have? _____

48 Who only has a dog? _____

B 25

3

49 In five years' time Annabelle will be 10.
How old was she three years ago? _____

50 In two years' time Jamie will be half the age of his sister,
who is 12 now. How old is Jamie now? _____

B 25

2

If D = 2, F = 4, H = 6, J = 12, and L = 24, give the answers to these calculations as letters.

51 D + D + D = _____

52 J – H = _____

53 D × D = _____

54 L ÷ J = _____

55 D × (H ÷ D) = _____

B 26

5

Change one word so that the sentence makes sense. Underline the word you are taking out and write your new word on the line.

B 14

Example   I waited in line to buy a <u>book</u> to see the film.   *ticket*

56 I went to the flower station to fill up my car for the long journey.   _____

57 Ellen took her sick hamster to the garage.   _____

58 The cat liked to sleep near the window to catch the
last of the moon's rays.   _____

59 The swan stretched its graceful, long foot as it floated in the pond.   _____

60 My favourite sort of ice marshmallow is chocolate.   _____

5

Solve the problems by working out the letter codes. The alphabet has been written out to help you.

B 24

A B C D E F G H I J K L M N O P Q R S T U V W X Y Z

61 In a code, FASTER is written as IDVWHU. How would you write RATES?_____

62 In a code, SPORT is written as URQTV. How would you write PLUM?   _____

63 In a code, MOST is written as NQVX. What does TCOI stand for?   _____

64 In a code, BEAN is written as DCCL. What does UFQU stand for?   _____

65 In a code, CREST is written as FUHVW. How would you write MASK?   _____

5

Now go to the Progress Chart to record your score!   Total   65

Paper 13

Look at these groups of words.

B 1

A	B	C	D
beef	orange	water	potato
lamb	pear	lemonade	cabbage
pork	cherry	coffee	pea

Choose the correct group for each of the words below. Write in the letter.

1 lemon   _____

2 spinach   _____

3 tea   _____

4 chicken   _____

5 grape   _____

5

Underline the two words, one from each group, which are closest in meaning.

Example (race, shop, <u>start</u>)　　(finish, <u>begin</u>, end)

6 (old, patterned, hunt)　　(new, search, faint)

7 (similar, opposite, wide)　　(afar, last, alike)

8 (out, back, overtake)　　(pass, front, in)

9 (show, contain, hide)　　(display, cry, guess)

10 (clean, tidy, vague)　　(sunny, explained, unclear)

B 3

5

Underline one word in the brackets which is most opposite in meaning to the word in capitals.

Example WIDE　　(broad　vague　long　<u>narrow</u>　motorway)

11 FAIL　　(work　point　pass　fade　call)

12 PEACE　　(quiet　softness　old　calm　conflict)

13 REPAIR　　(fix　push　damage　flatten　paint)

14 LEAD　　(chase　trail　pant　follow　hound)

15 CERTAIN　　(sure　absolute　positive　true　doubtful)

B 6

5

Underline the one word in the brackets which will go equally well with both the pairs of words outside the brackets.

Example rush, attack　　cost, fee　　(price, hasten, strike, <u>charge</u>, money)

16 pot, tin　　able, willing　　(box, well, metal, can, agreeable)

17 delicate, weightless　　ignite, flare　　(light, heavy, hot, dim, flat)

18 smack, strike　　success, chart-topper　　(pat, stroke, winning, hit, put)

19 light, shining　　able, clever　　(fired, ablaze, bright, cunning, lively)

20 elegant, stylish　　hurt, ache　　(neat, painful, tidy, paranoid, smart)

B 5

5

Find a word that can be put in front of each of the following words to make new, compound words.

Example cast　　fall　　ward　　pour　　*down*

21 house　　fly　　grocer　　finch　　＿＿＿＿

22 pecker　　worm　　cutter　　wind　　＿＿＿＿

23 place　　arm　　fighter　　side　　＿＿＿＿

24 bag　　shake　　rail　　writing　　＿＿＿＿

25 brush　　cut　　band　　dresser　　＿＿＿＿

B 11

5

Find the four-letter word hidden at the end of one word and the beginning of the next word. The order of the letters may not be changed.

B 21

Example   The children had bats and balls.   _sand_

26 All the boys and girls played sensibly at break-time.   _____

27 Alex was ready for his grand gala centenary celebrations.   _____

28 The famous actor never once forgot her lines.   _____

29 After my hard work, I was glad to have scored top in my class.   _____

30 I usually read for thirty minutes before I go to bed.   _____

5

Remove one letter from the word in capital letters to leave a new word. The meaning of the new word is given in the clue.

B 12

Example   AUNT   an insect   _ant_

31 MEAN   male   _____

32 STORE   painful   _____

33 PILOT   plan   _____

34 SHOP   jump   _____

35 TRIP   tear   _____

5

Find and underline the two words which need to change places for each sentence to make sense.

B 17

Example   She went to <u>letter</u> the <u>write</u>.

36 We put the cake in the bake to oven.

37 We put the names in alphabetical order so Bindy came before Annabel.

38 I sometimes count on my homework when doing my maths fingers.

39 The red rose is often white or wild in colour.

40 I have red seven pages in my read level book.

5

Find the letter which will end the first word and start the second word.

B 10

Example   peac (<u>h</u>) ome

41 star (___) arth

42 cras (___) all

43 hai (___) ail

44 pac (___) ear

45 el (___) new

5

Here are the number codes for five words. Match the right word to the right code.

BOOT	FALL	ALTO	TOOL	BAIL
3297	5117	3115	8277	2751

46 BOOT _____

47 FALL _____

48 ALTO _____

49 TOOL _____

50 BAIL _____

○ 5

Peter, David and Asif sit in a row in class. David is not beside Asif, who sits on the right of the three.

51 Who sits on the left? _____

52 Who is in the middle? _____

○ 2

53 In six years' time Alice will be twice as old as her sister, who is two now. How old will Alice be? _____

54 Four years ago Robert was five. In five years' time he will be half the age of his brother. How old is his brother now? _____

55 Town A is south of town B, east of town D and west of town F. Town C is north-east of town A. Which town is furthest west? _____

○ 3

Rearrange the letters in capitals to make another word. The new word has something to do with the first two words.

Example spot soil SAINT <u>STAIN</u>

56 twos doubles PARIS _____

57 goes out leaves EXIST _____

58 dressing gravy CAUSE _____

59 herb wise AGES _____

60 hazard risk GARDEN _____

○ 5

Change one word so that the sentence makes sense. Underline the word you are taking out and write your new word on the line.

B 14

> **Example**   I waited in line to buy a <u>book</u> to see the film.   <u>ticket</u>

61 The butcher had baked several cakes.   _____

62 Tame animals do not make very good pets.   _____

63 The bird had constructed a beautiful hole out of twigs.   _____

64 Sunday is the last month of the calendar year.   _____

65 The nurse asked her pupils to take their seats.   _____

5

Now go to the Progress Chart to record your score!   **Total**   65

Paper 14

Underline the pair of words most similar in meaning.

B 5

> **Example**   come, go   <u>roam, wander</u>   fear, fare

1 hurry, rest   swift, fast   break, fix

2 back, rear   hold, tie   under, over

3 polish, dirty   hunt, dog   miniature, small

4 shoot, score   aim, goal   wind, wave

5 take, give   prize, present   pole, rod

5

Underline the pair of words most opposite in meaning.

B 9

> **Example**   cup, mug   coffee, milk   <u>hot, cold</u>

6 wide, open   brilliant, dull   over, beyond

7 start, begin   fade, flatten   rude, polite

8 rise, fall   flake, drop   bounce, jump

9 post, join   criticise, praise   cry, wail

10 relaxed, tense   teach, instruct   lose, misplace

5

Underline the one word in the brackets which will go equally well with both the pairs of words outside the brackets.

Example   rush, attack   cost, fee   (price, hasten, strike, <u>charge</u>, money)

11 obvious, apparent   fields, grassland   (clear, plain, lawn, simple, ordinary)

12 elegance, beauty   prayer, thanks   (grace, amen, goodwill, attraction, power)

13 fill, arrange   bundle, parcel   (swell, gift, pack, place, pile)

14 particle, speck   cereal, seed   (piece, corn, bit, plant, grain)

15 sun, sky   celebrity, actor   (moon, star, shine, head, main)

○ 5

Find the letter which will complete both pairs of words, ending the first word and starting the second. The same letter must be used for both pairs of words.

Example   mea (t) able   fi (t) ub

16 star (——) ver   man (——) ntry

17 car   (——) angy   hin (——) umble

18 sa   (——) ame   ho   (——) rink

19 plan (——) ill   hun (——) nit

20 sou (——) ale   ram (——) rove

○ 5

Find the four-letter word hidden at the end of one word and the beginning of the next word. The order of the letters may not be changed.

Example   The children had bats and balls.   _sand_

21 Who let the cat in?   ————————

22 My dad's shed generally is rather messy.   ————————

23 Tremors from a severe earthquake can end up many miles away.   ————————

24 Fraser lent Sam a pencil because he'd left his at home.   ————————

25 I understand that aspirin deadens pain in the back.   ————————

○ 5

Change the first word into the last word, by changing one letter at a time and making a new, different word in the middle.

Example   CASE   _CASH_   LASH

26 PANT   ————   PARK

27 MOST   ————   MINT

28 SOUR   ————   SEAR

29 BEAT   ————   BRAG

30 NUTS   ————   CATS

○ 5

Look at the first group of three words. The word in the middle has been made from the other two words. Complete the second group of three words in the same way, making a new word in the middle of the group.

Example PAIN INTO TOOK   ALSO <u>SOON</u> ONLY

31	PALE	PEST	STIR	TAKE	_____	STOP
32	SOAR	OAST	TIME	SALE	_____	ONLY
33	FOOL	LOST	MAST	LEAP	_____	STAR
34	PRICE	RACE	PANIC	SPELT	_____	BISON
35	STEAM	LATE	CLEAR	TREND	_____	CREAM

Find the letter which will end the first word and start the second word.

Example   peac (<u>h</u>) ome

36 caree (___) ent

37 fir (___) dge

38 car (___) here

39 fee (___) rack

40 lam (___) arrel

Underline the two words, one from each group, which are closest in meaning.

Example   (race, shop, <u>start</u>)   (finish, <u>begin</u>, end)

41 (pound, paint, wash)   (beat, drop, destroy)

42 (lower, move, turn)   (raise, reduce, tear)

43 (mould, attach, injure)   (damage, remove, subtract)

44 (game, sickness, pattern)   (repair, chess, illness)

45 (knotty, spoilt, tough)   (weak, blessed, strong)

Find a word that can be put in front of each of the following words to make a new, compound word.

Example   cast   fall   ward   pour   <u>down</u>

46 lock   fare   lord   path   _____

47 fowl   front   logged   course   _____

48 proof   board   man   vane   _____

49 over   book   port   word   _____

50 ache   space   ground   pack   _____

54

Give the two missing pairs of letters and numbers. The alphabet has been written out to help you.

A B C D E F G H I J K L M N O P Q R S T U V W X Y Z

Example CQ DP EQ FP *GQ* HP

51 AL EL IM MM ____ ____

52 AA ZZ BB YY ____ ____

53 ZX XV VT TR ____ ____

54 NM NO ON OP ____ ____

55 A1 C2 E3 G4 ____ ____

◯ 5

If ← ↑ → ↓ ↔ Ⴘ ↑ is the code for REPLACE, what do these codes stand for?

B 24

56 → ↑ ↔ ← _____

57 Ⴘ ↓ ↔ → _____

58 → ↔ ↓ ↑ _____

59 ↓ ↑ ↑ ← _____

60 → ↔ ↓ ↔ Ⴘ ↑ _____

◯ 5

Change one word so that the sentence makes sense. Underline the word you are taking out and write your new word on the line.

B 14

Example I waited in line to buy a <u>book</u> to see the film. *ticket*

61 Mrs Stokes found that a glass of warm milk helped her wake at night. _____

62 One of Roger's guitar notes broke as he practised. _____

63 After being fatally wounded, the soldier was pronounced alive when he reached the hospital. _____

64 Watching the moon rise is a wonderful way to start the morning. _____

65 I was so hungry because I ate all of my dinner and then had a second helping. _____

◯ 5

Now go to the Progress Chart to record your score! Total ◯ 65

Paper 15

Underline the two words, one from each group, which are closest in meaning.

B 3

Example (race, shop, <u>start</u>) (finish, <u>begin</u>, end)

1 (speak, take, ask) (request, put, give)

2 (rough, shiny, clean) (wild, glistening, dirty)

3 (destroyed, repaired, reformed) (closed, compared, broken)

4 (cross, flighty, upset) (angry, cheerful, pale)

5 (drum, stick, noise) (tap, loud, music)

Underline the two words, one from each group, which are the most opposite in meaning.

    Example (dawn, <u>early</u>, wake) (<u>late</u>, stop, sunrise)

6 (shy, old, late) (aged, confident, true)

7 (cause, result, outcome) (effect, mistake, hide)

8 (follow, collect, light) (win, heavy, succeed)

9 (tired, controlled, hungry) (starving, thirsty, energetic)

10 (numb, hurting, rare) (painful, common, protected)

Find the letter which will end the first word and start the second word.

    Example peac (<u>h</u>) ome

11 pai (___) ule

12 fi (___) ase

13 too (___) ast

14 cove (___) ain

15 pun (___) oung

Find the four-letter word hidden at the end of one word and the beginning of the next word. The order of the letters may not be changed.

    Example The children had bats and balls. <u>sand</u>

16 You are lucky as it is the final one in the shop. _____

17 He considered the cash unnecessary in the circumstances. _____

18 The Incas taught us many interesting things. _____

19 The crowd quit cheering when the team lost the ball. _____

20 He ate the bag of sweets himself. _____

Which one letter can be added to the front of all these words to make new words?

    Example <u>c</u>are <u>c</u>at <u>c</u>rate <u>c</u>all

21 ___reak ___rand ___all ___oat

22 ___oat ___ool ___lean ___hain

23 ___ake   ___orn   ___oad   ___urn

24 ___ir   ___ate   ___ind   ___ault

25 ___ind   ___est   ___ould   ___hite

 5

Remove one letter from the word in capital letters to leave a new word. The meaning of the new word is given in the clue.

 B 12

    Example   AUNT   an insect   <u>ant</u>

26 DRAGOON   mythical beast   _____

27 COVER   bay   _____

28 ORATION   limited amount   _____

29 SHINE   leg   _____

30 METEOR   measuring instrument   _____

 5

Find and underline the two words which need to change places for each sentence to make sense.

 B 17

    Example   She went to <u>letter</u> the <u>write</u>.

31 The old track chugged along the endless train.

32 England is one of the largest counties in Kent.

33 I really enjoy classical films and black and white music.

34 It was very home so I ran briskly late.

35 The house was delivered to the wrong newspaper by mistake.

 5

Choose two words, one from each set of brackets, to complete the sentences in the best way.

 B 15

    Example   Tall is to (tree, <u>short</u>, colour) as narrow is to (thin, white, <u>wide</u>).

36 Speedy is to (fast, slow, late) as low is to (last, high, calm).

37 Ignore is to (overlook, welcome, accept) as praise is to (forget, change, honour).

38 Well is to (water, ill, better) as mine is to (wood, coal, wheat).

39 Damp is to (wet, sandy, dry) as cool is to (snow, rain, cold).

40 Kite is to (fly, sky, bird) as badger is to (nest, zoo, mammal).

 5

If A = 1, B = 4, D = 5, E = 10, S = 20, what are the sums of the following words by adding the letters together?

41 BAD = ⎯⎯⎯

42 SEED = ⎯⎯⎯

Give the answer to these calculations as letters.

43 S – E = ⎯⎯⎯

44 (A + B) + D = ⎯⎯⎯

45 E – D = ⎯⎯⎯

5

Find the letter which will complete both pairs of words, ending the first word and starting the second. The same letter must be used for both pairs of words.

Example   mea (t) able   fi (t) ub

46 clai (⎯) ost   cal (⎯) en

47 pra (⎯) olk   tr (⎯) oung

48 pac (⎯) nd   craz (⎯) ase

49 bal (⎯) ose   foo (⎯) eck

50 ful (⎯) oot   scraw (⎯) and

5

Rearrange the letters in capitals to make another word. The new word has something to do with the first two words.

Example   spot   soil   SAINT   STAIN

51 jump   hop   PALE   ⎯⎯⎯⎯

52 untrue   unreal   FLEAS   ⎯⎯⎯⎯

53 not strong fragile   WAKE   ⎯⎯⎯⎯

54 annoys   upsets   RANGES   ⎯⎯⎯⎯

55 fruit   canteloupe   LEMON   ⎯⎯⎯⎯

5

Change the first word into the last word, by changing one letter at a time and making a new, different word in the middle.

Example   CASE   CASH   LASH

56 POST   ⎯⎯⎯   PACT

57 MICE   ⎯⎯⎯   MATE

58 ARTS   ⎯⎯⎯   AIMS

59 SHIP   ⎯⎯⎯   SNAP

60 FLOW   ⎯⎯⎯   FLAT

5

Fill in the missing letters and numbers. The alphabet has been written out to help you.

A B C D E F G H I J K L M N O P Q R S T U V W X Y Z

Example AB is to CD as PQ is to <u>RS</u>.

61 DN is to BL as GQ is to _____.

62 BB is to YY as DD is to _____.

63 JJ is to LM as QQ is to _____.

64 ZY is to ZX as ZW is to _____.

65 A1 is to B2 as Y25 is to _____.

5

Now go to the Progress Chart to record your score!   Total   65

Progress Chart   Verbal Reasoning 9–10 years Book 2

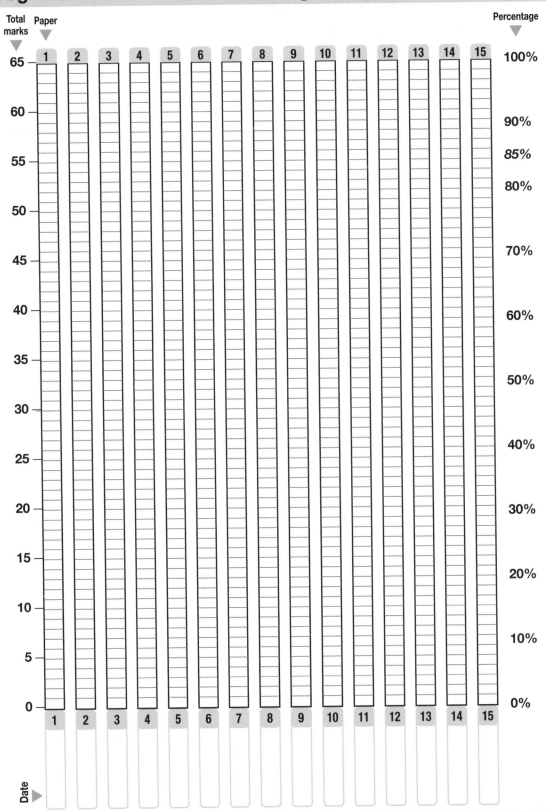

When you've finished the book use the Next Steps Planner